In these pages are 65 irresistible cookie sandwich recipes for every occasion, from classics with a twist to creative, sophisticated treats you haven't seen anywhere else. In just one bite, revisit your childhood with made-from-scratch Oreos, Milanos, and Nutter Butters—the list goes on! Wow your friends with a batch of Candy Cane Shortbread with Peppermint Buttercream at the next holiday cookie swap. For an elevated cocktail hour, enjoy a glass of chilled white wine alongside Parmesan Polenta Crackers with Chive Cream Cheese. You'll be baker of the year in your own home when you present your kids with Cookie Dough Ice Cream Brownie Sandwiches.

Here's the best part: A whole chapter dedicated to swirly buttercreams, smooth ganaches, fruity jams, and more lets you experiment with different cookie-filling pairings to your heart's content. Or leave out the filling altogether for a super simple bake. The possibilities are endless!

So don't wait—whip out those sheet pans and get your bake on. This book is *stuffed* with all the sweet and savory cookie recipes you'll ever need.

Stuffed

Stuf

— 65 —
mix & match
recipes

Whoopie Pies,
Macarons,
Ice Cream Sandwiches,
and More!

THE
SANDWICH COOKIE
BOOK

Heather Mubarak

CHRONICLE BOOKS
SAN FRANCISCO

Library of Congress Cataloging-in-Publication Data

Names: Mubarak, Heather, author.
Title: Stuffed : the sandwich cookie book / Heather Mubarak.
Description: San Francisco : Chronicle Books, 2023. | Includes index. |
    Identifiers: LCCN 2022040564 | ISBN 9781797214535
Subjects: LCSH: Cookies. | Baking. | LCGFT: Cookbooks.
Classification: LCC TX772 .M83 2023 | DDC 641.86/54--dc23/eng/20220830
LC record available at https://lccn.loc.gov/2022040564

Manufactured in China.

MIX
Paper | Supporting
responsible forestry
FSC™ C008047

Design by **LIZZIE VAUGHAN**.

Title hand lettering by **MONIQUE AIMEE**.

Typesetting by **FRANK BRAYTON**.

Typeset in Mont.

Bailey's Original Irish Cream is a registered trademark of R&A Bailey & Co; Chipwich is a registered trademark of Crave Better Foods, LLC; Everything but the Bagel is a registered trademark of Trader Joe's Company; Funfetti is a registered trademark of The J.M. Smucker Company; Heath is a registered trademark of Heath Ceramics; King Arthur is a registered trademark of King Arthur Baking Company, Inc.; Maldon is a registered trademark of Maldon Crystal Salt Company LLC; Milano is a registered trademark of Pepperidge Farm Incorporated; Nutella is a registered trademark of Ferrero S.P.A.; Nutter Butter is a registered trademark of Intercontinental Great Brands LLC; Oreo is a registered trademark of Intercontinental Great Brands LLC; Rodelle is a registered trademark of Archer-Daniels-Midland Company; Skor is a registered trademark of Hershey Chocolate & Confectionery LLC; Tootsie Roll is a registered trademark of Tootsie Roll Industries, LLC; Trader Joe's is a registered trademark of Trader Joe's Company.

10 9 8 7 6 5 4 3 2 1

Chronicle books and gifts are available at special quantity discounts to corporations, professional associations, literacy programs, and other organizations. For details and discount information, please contact our premiums department at corporatesales@chroniclebooks.com or at 1-800-759-0190.

Chronicle Books LLC
680 Second Street
San Francisco, California 94107
www.chroniclebooks.com

for my mom
who taught me early on that
home is where the cookies are.

and for my girls
I love you beyond measure.

CONTENTS

NO. 3　THE COOL COOKIES 105

NO. 4　TART & TANGY 157

NO. 5　COOKIES WITH A KICK 189

NO. 6   COCKTAIL COOKIES   217

NO. 7   THE FILLINGS   241

INTRODUCTION

THIS IS A BOOK FOR COOKIE LOVERS, WHICH PRETTY MUCH MEANS THIS IS A BOOK FOR EVERYONE IN THE WHOLE ENTIRE WORLD, BECAUSE WHO DOESN'T LOVE COOKIES?

As it does for many, my love for cookies goes way back to my happiest childhood memories. When I was in grade school, my mom would greet me and my sister on the front porch with a smile and a plate of freshly baked chocolate chip cookies warm from the oven. You know the ones. Straight from the recipe on the bright yellow bag and baked with love by Mom herself. I have always loved cookies more than any other dessert. Ever since I can recall, an ooey-gooey, soft and chewy chocolate chip cookie has been my favorite indulgence. The simpler, the better. A cookie is the one treat I cannot live without.

Thanks to Mom, I grew up with a serious sweet tooth, and I have been making a career out of all things sweet for as long as I can remember. After starting a hand-crafted almond toffee business using a secret family recipe, I became known to many as the "toffee lady." And my signature brown butter blondies have won over hundreds of sugar-starved third graders at school bake sales. I will be forever proud of my lazy girl snack cakes, and I will never run out of ways to reinvent the classic Bundt.

But the treat I love to bake (and eat!) the most is a pretty little sandwich cookie. There is a sandwich cookie for every mood, every special occasion, every craving. When it comes to cookies, two is always better than one, if you ask me. And what's not to love about a pair of delicious cookies smooshed together with swirls of fluffy buttercream, scoops of homemade ice cream, or spoonfuls of chocolate filling in the middle? As you turn the pages of this book, you will wonder where these double-doozy cookies have been all your life. From Wannabe Brownie Cookies with Peanut Butter Frosting (page 67) and Strawberry Shortcake Macarons (page 185) to Chocolate-Dipped Peanut Butter Cookie Ice Cream Sandwiches (page 119), these stuffed cookies will quickly become fast favorites that you will make again and again.

Everyone has a favorite cookie flavor, whether it is rich and chocolatey, light and buttery, or sweet and salty. With cravings top of mind, the cookie recipes are organized into six chapters: Oldies but Goodies, For the Love of Chocolate, The Cool Cookies, Tart & Tangy, Cookies with a Kick, and

Cocktail Cookies. Each chapter includes a collection of all kinds of cookies, whether simple, elevated versions of cherished childhood classics suitable for a weeknight dessert, or elegant favorites perfect for any party. There is also a smattering of quick and easy recipes that are must-haves for when the cookie craving strikes, no special occasion needed. Within these pages you'll find no-fuss cookies to make every day along with fancier cookies to make every so often. Each of these cookies is crave-worthy on its own, but when paired with the perfect filling, it is over-the-top delicious. Because no two cookie lovers are alike, I have written this book as a choose-your-own-adventure of sorts. Each of the cookies can be baked and enjoyed as they are, or they can be paired in endless combinations with the buttercreams, fillings, ice creams, and frostings found in the final chapter of the book.

My three daughters—the very best taste testers a baker could ask for—have inherited my cookie-a-day philosophy. Just as I was, my girls have been brought up baking by their mother's side. Through our days together in the kitchen, I have taught them to keep their hearts full and the cookie jar even fuller. Each of these recipes is tried-and-true, one hundred percent loved by the most discerning of palates. The recipes are accessible enough for the novice baker, while more advanced cookie makers will appreciate the chance to expand their skills (hello, Hot Fudge Sundae Macarons [page 85]!). I want bakers of all skill levels to be inspired to make delicious, bakery-worthy batches of cookies at home.

If you are holding this book, I'm guessing you are also a self-declared cookie lover. Nice to meet you! Since we are doing introductions, you should know that I am a self-taught baker who learned everything she knows from good ol' fashioned trial and error. I spent many years running a confectionary business, which taught me everything I need to know about preparation and production. And through the blog, *Browned Butter Blondie*, which I started a few years ago, I've learned how to write recipes that inspire home bakers to get creative in the kitchen and give them the confidence to try something new.

A handful of the recipes you see here are favorites from the blog, but most are never-before-seen cookies with that extra something special that will keep you coming back for seconds (and thirds!). Each recipe comes with loads of tips and tricks that guarantee the very best sandwich cookies every time. My hope is that the pages of this book become dog-eared and chocolate stained, and that these recipes fill your cookie jars and freezer shelves and are one day passed down to your cookie-loving kids.

Happy Baking!

THIRTEEN TOOLS FOR SANDWICH COOKIE SUCCESS

Don't think of these tools as essentials necessarily. Truth be told, you don't need much more than a bowl and a spoon to make cookies, but investing in some of these items will make your cookies the best they can be.

1.

Baking sheets

Whether you are using Grandma's old battered baking sheet or a shiny new model, the best ones are made of aluminum and come in a half-sheet size that measures 13 by 18 in [33 by 46 cm]. Choose one with a reinforced rim to help contain spills and crumbs. No need to pay extra for fancy bells and whistles. The keep-it-simple principle definitely applies to baking sheets—basic is best.

2.

Kitchen scale

Because baking is a science, measuring ingredients inaccurately can make or break a recipe. Take all the guesswork out of baking by using a digital scale to ensure that all of your measurements are precise. I also use a scale to weigh scoops of cookie dough so they bake up equal in size.

3.

Cookie scoop

A cookie scoop is a great tool for creating consistent and uniform cookies. Since sandwich cookies are all about pairing up two cookies of the same size, a good cookie scoop will prove very useful when it comes time to dole out the dough. Cookie scoops come in a variety of sizes. If you like to bake teeny, tiny cookies, reach for a 2 teaspoon cookie scoop. For large and in-charge cookies, I like to use a 3 tablespoon scoop. Opt for one with a spring-loaded lever that is made with high-quality stainless steel.

4.

Rolling pin

Every good baker needs a great rolling pin. I use mine constantly for rolling out Gingerbread Cookies (see page 207) and Chocolate Pinwheel Cookies (see page 73), among other treats. Rolling pins come in various styles and materials, but I have had the most success with a simple French marble one with tapered ends. It's easy to use and helps keep the dough chilled while you work.

5.

Silicone baking mat

Silicone baking mats are used to line baking sheets to create an even, nonstick surface. Since you can wash and reuse them repeatedly, they get bonus points for sustainability. I especially love using silicone mats with printed templates for making macarons, as it provides an easy visual guide for making cookies equal in size.

6.
Parchment paper

For picture-perfect cookies every time, stock up on parchment paper. Like a silicone baking mat, parchment paper is also coated in silicone, which promotes even baking and makes cleanup a breeze. By using a sheet of parchment on top of your baking sheet, you'll reduce the wear and tear on your bakeware. I also use parchment to line the pan when baking bars or brownies to help with easy removal and cutting once baked. And it comes in handy when rolling out cut-out cookie dough. No need to throw parchment paper out after the first use—reuse it over and over until it's tattered and torn.

7.
Oven thermometer

If there is one thing I've learned in all of my years of baking, it's that no two ovens are created equal. Every oven runs differently and no two are the same. A simple oven thermometer is an easy way to tell how hot—or how cold—your oven is running. Position it on the center rack of your oven and adjust your baking temperature as needed. Keep in mind that most ovenproof thermometers are relatively

inexpensive and do wear out over time. I set a calendar reminder to replace mine once a year.

8.
Cookie cutters

A set of heavy-duty, sharp-edged cookie cutters is essential for perfectly shaped cut-out cookies. Biscuit cutters can double as cookie cutters too. I love the ones with dainty scalloped edges for the prettiest sandwich cookies.

9.
Hand or stand mixer

Most of the recipes in this book call for a stand mixer. With plenty of power and capacity to whip up all of your favorite doughs, frostings, and fillings, a sturdy stand mixer is a worthwhile investment. If you bake only on occasion or don't have the counter space for another appliance, a portable hand-held electric mixer or trusty wooden spoon will get the job done.

10.
Piping bag and tips

To add that extra bit of fancy to your sandwich cookies, I recommend purchasing a handful of piping tips in various sizes. A medium plain round tip is perfect for piping macarons, while a larger star tip will create beautiful swirls of frosting. Piping bags are

available in cloth or plastic. Use whichever material you prefer, but stick with the larger bags, since the smaller ones are easy to overfill, making cookie sandwich assembly a messy endeavor.

11.
Sifter

A sifter is essential when a recipe calls for sifting flour, cocoa powder, or confectioners' sugar. It also comes in handy for decorating the tops of cookies with a sprinkle of sugar. If you don't have an actual sifter, a fine-mesh strainer will do the trick.

12.
Wire cooling rack

A wire cooling rack is helpful for cooling cookies quickly, and the extra airflow around the cookies keeps them crisp on the bottom. Use a wire cooling rack over the top of a baking sheet to catch drizzles and drips when dusting cookies with sugar or piping on melted chocolate.

13.
Ruler

A simple plastic or metal ruler will help with cutting picture-perfect squares of bars or brownies, and slice 'n' bakes of even widths. This will come in handy more often than you think.

PANTRY MUST-HAVES FOR COOKIE BAKING

Stock your pantry with these baking basics for delicious cookies whenever the craving strikes. Most of the ingredients listed are readily available at your local market or can be found online.

1.
Butter

All the recipes in this book call for unsalted Grade AA butter. This allows you to control the amount of salt that is added to a recipe. Unsalted butter stocked on grocery store shelves is typically freshest because salt acts as a preservative, which lengthens the shelf life. That said, if you have only salted butter on hand, you can always reduce or omit the added salt in the recipe. You won't find European-style butter listed in any of the recipes here. The higher fat content of European-style butter can lead to excess spreading of the dough and a greasier texture that I don't care for in my cookies. Save it for spreading on your morning toast or waffles.

2.
Flour

The recipes that call for all-purpose flour were tested with King Arthur Baking unbleached all-purpose flour. A smattering of recipes contain bread flour as well. If you've never baked cookies with bread flour before, you'll be pleasantly surprised at the added texture and chew it provides. A handful of recipes contain almond flour, which is found alongside regular flour in the baking aisle of most major grocery stores. It's important to look for almond flour that is blanched and finely ground. I highly recommend measuring your flour with a digital scale for best results. If measuring without a scale, use the spoon-and-level method. Begin by fluffing the flour in the bag or canister with a fork. Then use a large spoon to transfer the flour into a measuring cup, being careful not to pack it down. Overfill the cup slightly and then use the flat edge of a knife to level and sweep the excess flour off the top. If you scoop the flour by dipping the measuring cup into a bag or canister of flour, also known as the scoop-and-level method, you risk packing the flour in too densely. Too much flour can result in dry cookies that do not spread properly in the oven.

GLUTEN-FREE FLOUR

While the taste and texture will differ slightly, virtually any cookie in this book can be made gluten-free by replacing the flour. Replace the flour in the recipe cup-for-cup with the gluten-free flour. If you use 1 cup of regular all-purpose flour, you will use 1 cup of gluten-free flour. In addition, you'll need to add ¼ teaspoon xanthan gum per

1 cup of flour. Alternatively, you can use a gluten-free flour blend that already contains xanthan gum. Because gluten helps hold the matrix of a cookie together, gluten-free cookies often spread too much. To counteract this, use cold butter rather than room-temperature butter and be careful not to overbake. Gluten-free cookies tend to be drier, so they will not stay fresh as long as traditional cookies.

3.
Sugar

Most of the cookies in this book contain both regular granulated sugar and brown sugar. Granulated sugar is standard, but I also love baking with superfine baker's sugar. It's simply granulated sugar that has been ground to a finer texture. Most grocery stores carry both products, but you can make your own by pulsing regular granulated sugar in a food processor fitted with a blade attachment. For brown sugar, use light brown unless dark brown sugar is specified in the recipe. Confectioners' sugar, also called powdered sugar, is another common ingredient in this book. Sift confectioners' sugar first to eliminate any lumps and bumps.

4.
Eggs

As a rule, the recipes you see here use room-temperature Grade A large eggs. I like to set my eggs out at least an hour before baking, but in a pinch you can place them in a bowl of warm water for 10 minutes to bring them to room temperature.

5.
Chocolate

There's no shortage of chocolate here—bittersweet, semisweet, milk, dark, white, unsweetened . . . we use it all! They are all somewhat interchangeable and my best advice would be to get the highest-quality chocolate you can. It matters! Good chocolate should have a rich flavor and a smooth finish. If you don't love the taste of the chocolate before you mix it into the cookie dough, you won't love the cookie once it's baked. As a rule, I don't bake cookies using chocolate that is over 72 percent cacao. Anything over that is a bit too bitter for my taste. Always choose white chocolate that is made from real cocoa butter and has no added fats or fillers. I like to melt chocolate using a double boiler. No need to invest in a fancy piece of equipment. You can DIY your own double boiler using a medium pot and a heatproof glass bowl. It works great for melting chocolate over gentle, indirect heat.

6.
Cocoa powder

There are two types of cocoa powder: Dutch-process and unsweetened. Dutch-process is darker in color, smoother in finish, and less acidic. Most of the recipes you find here call for Dutch-process cocoa powder. Unless specified, do not substitute unsweetened cocoa powder.

7.
Vanilla

The recipes in this book use pure vanilla extract. A high-quality vanilla is worth splurging on. I prefer Rodelle Gourmet Pure Vanilla Extract. Steer clear of anything labeled "artificial."

8.
Salt

Salt enhances the flavor of butter and flour in baked goods and works magic in recipes with chocolate. The recipes in this book call for table salt, kosher salt, and fine sea salt. You likely already have table salt in your pantry as it's the most common type; in the recipes, I refer to it simply as "salt." Kosher and sea salt both come in larger, coarser grains and have a milder flavor than table salt. If substituting table salt for kosher or sea salt, use half the amount called for in the recipe. Sprinkle finishing salt, also called fleur de sel or flaky sea salt, on top of

baked cookies for a pop of flavor. It's optional, but try it once and you'll be hooked!

9.
Spices

A handful of recipes in the book call for ground spices such as cinnamon, cardamom, nutmeg, allspice, ginger, and cloves. If you bake with these spices only every so often, keep in mind that while they may appear to last a lifetime, they actually have a shelf life of 6 months to a year. Pro tip: Label your spice bottles with the date of purchase and refresh your stock as needed.

10.
Leavening agents

Leavening agents, namely baking powder and baking soda, produce gas inside cookie dough, which causes it to expand. Without the addition of leavening agents, cookies will fall flatter than a pancake. Keep in mind that these chemical leavening agents lose potency over time and should be replaced before they expire.

WITH THE COOKIES, FILLINGS, AND FROSTINGS IN THESE PAGES, YOU'LL HAVE EVERYTHING YOU NEED TO BAKE UNBELIEVABLY DELICIOUS SANDWICH COOKIES.

Each recipe in this book is written in detail to ensure that your sandwich cookies look great and taste even better. Before we get started, to help you master the art of cookie making, I've put together a list of tips and tricks to help you bake the perfect batch every time.

The Basics of Baking Cookies

Know your oven

It's important to not only preheat your oven, but also to check that the temperature is accurate. I heard another baker once say that ovens are just like people: They come in all shapes and sizes and no two are the same. Use an oven thermometer to check if your oven is running too hot or too cold. Inaccurate oven temperature could lead to your cookies spreading too much or not enough, which can alter both their texture and taste. For most recipes, I give a range for bake time. If your oven runs hot, check the cookies at the lower end of the range. If your oven runs cool, expect the cookies to take longer to bake. As a general rule, the instructions advise pulling the cookies from the oven when the edges are just set and the centers are still soft and slightly underbaked. This is because as the cookies cool, the residual heat from the baking sheet continues to bake the cookies. To avoid dry, brittle cookies, always err on the side of underbaking rather than overbaking.

Prepare your pans

For easy removal of the baked cookies, always line your baking sheets with parchment paper or a silicone baking mat. Bonus: It makes cleanup a breeze! For evenly baked cookies, always allow your sheets to cool to room temperature between batches. It's helpful to have two baking sheets so you have one to use while the other is cooling.

Use room-temperature butter

There are just a handful of recipes in this book that call for cold butter straight from the refrigerator. Most often I call for butter that has been softened to room temperature.

Room-temperature butter should be ever-so-slightly cool to the touch and soft enough that pressing gently with your finger leaves a small indentation. When in doubt, err on the side of the butter being slightly colder, as the mixer will warm the butter as it beats. Only use melted butter when it's called for. And if a recipe calls for browned butter, trust me, it's worth it! Cookies are all about the butter, so follow these rules and you'll be golden.

Measure your ingredients correctly

I'm about the laziest baker there is, but believe me when I say that measuring your ingredients properly makes all the difference. If you don't have a kitchen scale, measure your dry ingredients carefully using the spoon-and-level method. Use a spoon to scoop the dry ingredients (flour, cocoa powder, etc.) into a measuring cup. Do not pack the ingredients down unless measuring brown sugar. Next, use the back of a knife to tap along the top of the measuring cup and then run the knife across the top to level the ingredients. Measure liquid ingredients using a glass measuring cup and smaller quantities of ingredients with measuring spoons. I know, I know . . . more dishes to wash, but it's a small price to pay for perfect cookies every time.

Do not overmix the dough

Most cookie dough needs a gentle touch, so don't plan on squeezing in a good arm workout while making these recipes. Because overmixing your dough causes the gluten in the flour to activate, it's best to keep the mixing to a minimum. Mix the dough only until a few streaks of flour remain, and always stir in extras like chocolate chips and nuts by hand with a wooden spoon or spatula.

Cool the cookies completely before adding fillings

Warm cookies and chilled frostings, fillings, and curds don't mix, so be sure to cool the cookies completely on a wire cooling rack before assembling your sandwiches. To speed up the process a bit, pop the cookies into the refrigerator or freezer for a few minutes until they are cool to the touch. Many of the recipes call for chilling the sandwich cookies once assembled, so clear some space in the refrigerator or freezer ahead of time.

- **Prep your ingredients ahead of time.** Making perfect macarons is a combination of precision and practice. Each individual step moves quickly, and having all of your ingredients measured and in place ahead of time is key.
- **Measure the ingredients using a digital kitchen scale.** Accuracy is the name of the game when it comes to macaron success. Because precise measurements are essential to the outcome, I have not included cup measurements, which leave too much room for error. Always measure the ingredients by weight—it makes all the difference!

- **Sift, sift, and sift again.** Sift your dry ingredients at least three times for a smooth, lump-free batter.
- **Use an oven thermometer.** Baking temperature is crucial to successful macaron making. I highly recommend purchasing an inexpensive oven thermometer to check your oven's accuracy. It's a small investment that goes a long way.
- **Do not overmix the macaron batter.** First, be sure to fold rather than stir the batter. Stop mixing once you can draw a figure 8 with the batter without it breaking away from the spatula.

- **Use a silicone baking mat with printed macaron templates.** This will take all the guesswork out of piping the batter. Just use the template as your guide.
- **Dry the macarons before baking.** The batter must rest at room temperature in order to bake properly and create the macarons' signature "feet." The macarons are ready to bake when they are dry to the touch. This can take anywhere from 30 minutes to several hours depending on the temperature in your kitchen and even *the weather*. Yes, the weather! I told you these were one finicky cookie. But done right, they are magical.

A Few More Thoughts

Follow the recipe

Before starting, I suggest reading through the recipe twice to be sure you have all the ingredients, equipment, and allotted time (including for chilling the dough) to bake and assemble the sandwich cookies. If you skip ahead too quickly, you'll miss all the helpful nuggets of information I share along the way.

Let's talk swaps

I always suggest following a recipe as it is written for best success. You won't get the same result if you change the ingredients, measurements, or methods of the recipe. It's that simple, folks. But I do give you full permission to swap the fillings to your heart's content. Don't love milk chocolate ganache? No biggie. Use dark chocolate. Not a fan of cherries? I get it. Swap in raspberry jam instead. While each cookie comes with a recommended filling, the recipes in this book are meant to cater to your individual cookie cravings. Feel free to follow your sweet tooth and mix and match cookies and fillings however you see fit. The final chapter features recipes for all the frostings, ganaches, curds, and ice creams, which can be paired with any of the cookies. Use the handy Mix & Match boxes to inspire you to come up with your own delicious pairings.

Make-ahead icons

Throughout the book, you'll see snowflake icons alongside some of the recipes on the top left of the page. This indicates that the dough or the cookies themselves have to be chilled for at least an hour. Plan ahead and be sure you have enough time.

Freezer stash

Ah, the almighty freezer stash. I'm not sure there is anything better than finding a container of Gingerdoodle Neapolitan Cookie dough (page 203) or a ready-to-eat Peanut Butter Pretzel Cookie ice cream sandwich (page 123) stashed away in the freezer when you're looking for the perfect midday pick-me-up or late-night snack. Most of the recipes in this book can be made ahead and frozen to be enjoyed later. Some of the cookies will need to be frozen without filling and others will benefit from a little chill time once the cookies and fillings have been sandwiched together. Be sure to wrap the cookies and keep them tightly covered, protecting them from odors and air. Properly stored, they will last for months in the freezer.

Storing cookies

Always store cookies once they are completely cool, never warm. Stack in an airtight container or plastic bag between layers of parchment paper. If making a variety of cookies, be sure to store crispy cookies such as shortbread or Homemade Milanos (page 51) separately from soft cookies like Oatmeal Cream Pies (page 29). This keeps the moisture from the soft and chewy cookies from softening the crispier ones.

Shipping cookies

Many of the cookies in this book package up well for shipping off to family and friends near and far. For the perfect gift that keeps on giving, choose a sturdy cookie and snuggle them into a lightweight metal container with layers of bubble wrap and parchment paper. Use extra parchment or wax paper to fill in any spaces so that the cookies are packed tightly into the tin, leaving little wiggle room to move around in transit.

A NOTE FROM ONE COOKIE LOVER TO ANOTHER . . .

Cookie lovers, I am thrilled that this book has found its way into your hands. My hope is that these are the recipes you'll use to celebrate life's sweetest occasions, take to picnics and potlucks, and share with family and friends for years to come. I've tinkered with these recipes for years—partly to satisfy my own cravings, but mostly to share with the people I love. And now that you have this book, you can bake them too! As you bake your way through the recipes, remember: Your cookies don't need to be picture-perfect to be delicious. My goal is that you will find each of these recipes as fun to make as it is to eat. And on that note, let the baking begin!

OLDIES
BUT GOODIES

CLASSIC CHOCOLATE CHIP COOKIES
WITH
VANILLA BUTTERCREAM

CHOCOLATE CHIP COOKIES

1 cup plus 2 tablespoons [140 g] all-purpose flour, spooned and leveled

1 cup [125 g] bread flour or more all-purpose flour, spooned and leveled

1 teaspoon baking soda

¾ teaspoon salt

1 cup [226 g] unsalted butter, at room temperature

¾ cup [150 g] light brown sugar, packed

¼ cup plus 3 tablespoons [95 g] granulated sugar

1 egg, at room temperature

1½ teaspoons vanilla extract

1¼ cups [225 g] semisweet chocolate chips

FOR ASSEMBLY

1 recipe Vanilla Buttercream (page 246)

Try as I might, I'm still that girl that's always late to the party. But I always bring dessert. Most of the time I show up with a batch of these classic chocolate chippers. These are those cookies that make people go "ohhmmmgee, who made these?" And since I know you're going to ask, the answer is yes. You really do need to chill the dough. #worthit

TO MAKE THE COOKIES

In a medium bowl, whisk together the all-purpose flour, bread flour, baking soda, and salt. Set aside.

In the bowl of a stand mixer fitted with the paddle attachment, cream together the butter, brown sugar, and granulated sugar on medium-high speed for 3 to 4 minutes, or until light and fluffy. Stop the mixer and scrape down the sides of the bowl. Add the egg and vanilla, mixing on low speed until fully incorporated. Stop the mixer and scrape down the sides of the bowl once more. Add the flour mixture to the butter mixture in two additions. Mix on low speed just until combined. Do not overmix. Remove the bowl from the mixer and stir in the chocolate chips using a spatula or wooden spoon.

Cover the bowl with plastic wrap and chill overnight.

cont.

Once the dough is chilled, preheat the oven to 350°F [180°C]. Line two baking sheets with parchment paper or silicone baking mats. Using a 2 tablespoon cookie scoop, place scoops of dough 2 in [5 cm] apart on the prepared baking sheets. Bake for 8 to 10 minutes, or until the edges are golden brown. The centers may look slightly underbaked but the cookies will continue to bake once removed from the oven.

Allow the cookies to cool on the baking sheets for 5 minutes before using a spatula to carefully transfer them to a wire cooling rack. Let cool completely before adding the buttercream.

TO ASSEMBLE THE COOKIE SANDWICHES
Transfer the Vanilla Buttercream to a piping bag. Swirl the buttercream onto the flat underside of one cookie. Top with a second cookie, flat-side down, and gently press together. Repeat with the remaining cookies until all the sandwiches are assembled.

Store cookies (without filling) in a cool, dry place, tightly covered, for up to 3 days. Once assembled, these are best eaten day of, but they also freeze beautifully. Wrap them tightly in plastic wrap and store in a freezer bag for up to 2 months. Defrost at room temperature before serving.

OATMEAL CREAM PIES
WITH
BROWN SUGAR BUTTERCREAM

OATMEAL COOKIES

¾ cup [75 g] quick oats

¾ cup [95 g] all-purpose flour, spooned and leveled

¾ cup [95 g] bread flour, spooned and leveled

1 teaspoon baking soda

¾ teaspoon kosher salt

¾ teaspoon ground cinnamon

⅛ teaspoon ground nutmeg

1 cup [226 g] unsalted butter, at room temperature

1 cup [200 g] light brown sugar, packed

½ cup [100 g] granulated sugar

1 tablespoon molasses (not blackstrap)

1½ teaspoons vanilla extract

1 egg plus 1 egg yolk, at room temperature

FOR ASSEMBLY

1 recipe Brown Sugar Buttercream (page 252)

These oatmeal cookies give me all the warm fuzzies. They are soft and chewy and perfectly spiced. And the brown sugar buttercream . . . don't even get me started. I make these cookies year-round, but I especially love them in the fall when the weather starts to turn.

TO MAKE THE COOKIES
In a medium bowl, whisk together the oats, all-purpose flour, bread flour, baking soda, salt, cinnamon, and nutmeg. Set aside.

In the bowl of a stand mixer fitted with the paddle attachment, mix the butter, brown sugar, and granulated sugar on medium speed until combined. Stop the mixer, scrape down the sides of the bowl, increase the speed to medium-high, and beat until light and fluffy, about 2 minutes. Turn the mixer speed to low and add the molasses and vanilla. Once combined, add the egg and egg yolk, one at a time, waiting until the first is fully incorporated before adding the second. Stop the mixer and scrape down the sides of the bowl. Add the oats mixture in two additions, mixing until just combined. Do not overmix.

Cover the bowl and chill the dough for at least 3 hours or overnight.

cont.

Once the dough is chilled, preheat the oven to 350°F [180°C]. Line two baking sheets with parchment paper or silicone baking mats.

Using a 2 tablespoon cookie scoop, place scoops of dough 2 in [5 cm] apart on the prepared baking sheets. Bake for 10 to 11 minutes, or until the edges are golden brown and the centers are just set.

Allow the cookies to cool on the baking sheets for 5 minutes before using a spatula to carefully transfer them to a wire cooling rack to cool completely.

TO ASSEMBLE THE COOKIE SANDWICHES
Transfer the Brown Sugar Buttercream to a piping bag. Pipe about 3 tablespoons of the buttercream onto the flat underside of one cookie. Top with a second cookie, flat-side down, and gently press together. Repeat with the remaining cookies until all the sandwiches are assembled.

Store tightly wrapped in a cool, dry place for up to 3 days.

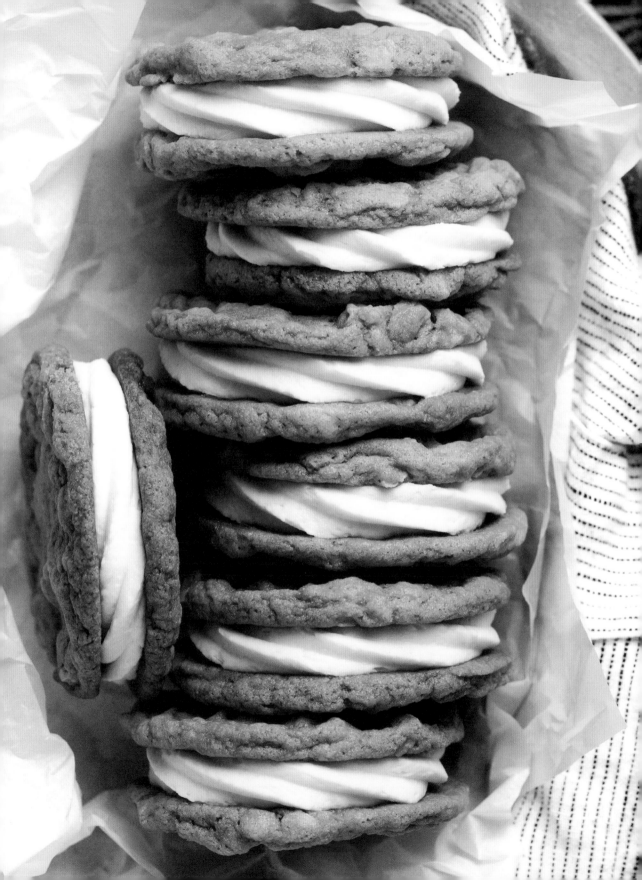

FUNFETTI COOKIES
WITH
CAKE BATTER BUTTERCREAM

FUNFETTI COOKIES

2¼ cups [280 g] all-purpose flour, spooned and leveled

1 teaspoon cornstarch

¾ teaspoon baking soda

½ teaspoon salt

¾ cup [170 g] unsalted butter, cold and cubed

1 cup [200 g] granulated sugar

¼ cup [50 g] light brown sugar, packed

1 egg, at room temperature

1 teaspoon vanilla extract (use clear vanilla extract if possible)

⅓ cup [55 g] rainbow sprinkles

FOR ASSEMBLY

1 recipe Cake Batter Buttercream (page 249)

These fun and festive sugar cookies make every day feel like a party. While I love them stuffed with vanilla ice cream, they're especially good with birthday cake–flavored buttercream. They're on the sweet side, so feel free to scale back on the sprinkles as you see fit. If you have a budding baker in the house, this is the perfect recipe to introduce them to the magic of rainbow sprinkles.

TO MAKE THE COOKIES
Preheat the oven to 350°F [180°C]. Line two baking sheets with parchment paper or silicone baking mats. Set aside.

In a medium bowl, whisk together the flour, cornstarch, baking soda, and salt. Set aside.

In the bowl of a stand mixer fitted with the paddle attachment, cream together the butter, granulated sugar, and brown sugar on medium-high speed until well combined, 2 to 3 minutes. Stop the mixer and scrape down the sides of the bowl. Add the egg and vanilla. Mix on low speed until fully incorporated. Add the flour mixture in two additions and mix on low speed until combined. Do not overmix.

Remove the bowl from the stand mixer and stir in the rainbow sprinkles by hand with a spatula or wooden spoon, being careful not to overmix the dough.

cont.

Using a 2 tablespoon cookie scoop, scoop out the dough and roll into uniform balls using your hands. Place the dough balls on the prepared baking sheets, spacing them 2 in [5 cm] apart.

Bake the cookies for 10 to 11 minutes, or until the edges are barely golden brown and the tops are cracked but still slightly underbaked.

Remove the pans from the oven and allow the cookies to cool on the baking sheets for 5 minutes before using a spatula to carefully transfer them to a wire cooling rack to cool completely.

TO ASSEMBLE THE COOKIE SANDWICHES

Transfer the Cake Batter Buttercream to a piping bag fitted with a large star tip. Pipe a swirl of frosting onto the flat underside of one cookie. Top with a second cookie, flat-side down, and gently press together. Repeat with the remaining cookies until all the sandwiches are assembled. If the buttercream is soft, place the cookie sandwiches in the refrigerator to set for 20 minutes.

Store the cookie sandwiches tightly covered in the refrigerator for up to 3 days. Bring to room temperature for 20 to 30 minutes before serving.

PEANUT BUTTER COOKIES
WITH
PEANUT BUTTER MOUSSE
AND CHOCOLATE GANACHE

PEANUT BUTTER COOKIES

1½ cups plus 2 tablespoons [205 g] all-purpose flour, spooned and leveled

¾ teaspoon baking soda

¼ teaspoon kosher salt

¾ cup [220 g] creamy peanut butter, at room temperature

½ cup [113 g] unsalted butter, at room temperature

¾ cup [150 g] light brown sugar, packed

⅓ cup [65 g] granulated sugar, plus 2 tablespoons for rolling

1 egg, at room temperature

1 teaspoon vanilla extract

Flaky sea salt, for sprinkling (optional)

FOR ASSEMBLY

1 recipe Chocolate Ganache made with milk chocolate (page 245)

1 recipe Peanut Butter Mousse (page 255)

Peanut butter cookies are serious business in our house-hold. My husband isn't a big sweets fan, but he never says no to a good peanut butter cookie. So I took his all-time favorite peanut butter cookie to the next level and added a dollop of milk chocolate ganache and a hefty swirl of creamy peanut butter mousse. They're lights-out deli-cious! Serve them straight from the fridge or freezer with a sprinkle of flaky sea salt. You can't go wrong.

TO MAKE THE COOKIES

Preheat the oven to 350°F [180°C]. Line two baking sheets with parchment paper or silicone baking mats.

In a medium bowl, combine the flour, baking soda, and salt. Whisk together and set aside.

In the bowl of a stand mixer fitted with the paddle attachment, cream together the peanut butter, butter, brown sugar, and ⅓ cup [65 g] of the granulated sugar on medium-high speed until light and creamy, about 2 minutes. Add the egg and vanilla and mix on medium speed until well combined. Add the flour mixture and mix on low speed until just combined. Do not overmix the dough.

cont.

Place the remaining 2 tablespoons of granulated sugar in a small bowl. Using a 3 tablespoon cookie scoop, scoop the dough into about 2 oz [55 g] portions and roll each between your hands to form a uniform ball. Roll each cookie dough ball in the sugar to coat.

Place the dough balls 2 to 3 in [5 to 7.5 cm] apart on the prepared baking sheets. Use the tines of a fork to press down on the top of each cookie, flattening them about halfway and making a crosshatch pattern on top. Bake for 8 to 9 minutes, or until the cookies begin to crack on top and the edges are barely set.

Let the cookies cool on the baking sheets for 5 minutes before using a spatula to carefully transfer them to a wire cooling rack to cool completely before assembling the sandwiches. Sprinkle with flaky sea salt, if desired.

TO ASSEMBLE THE COOKIE SANDWICHES
Turn half of the cookies over, flat-side up. Place 1 or 2 teaspoons of the Chocolate Ganache on the flat side of the cookies, spreading almost to the edges.

Add the Peanut Butter Mousse to a piping bag. Pipe a swirl of the mousse on top of the ganache. Top each with a second cookie, flat-side down, and gently press together. Place the cookie sandwiches in the refrigerator for 30 minutes to set.

Store the cookie sandwiches tightly covered in the refrigerator for up to 3 days.

COPYCAT NUTTER BUTTER COOKIES

COPYCAT NUTTER BUTTERS

1½ cups [190 g] all-purpose flour, spooned and leveled

½ teaspoon baking powder

¾ cup [220 g] creamy, natural peanut butter (see Note)

6 tablespoons [85 g] unsalted butter, at room temperature

½ cup [100 g] light brown sugar, packed

¼ cup [50 g] granulated sugar

1 teaspoon vanilla extract

1 to 2 tablespoons whole milk (optional, depending on dough consistency)

FOR ASSEMBLY

1 recipe Peanut Butter Filling (page 256)

These Nutter Butter knockoffs are a bit softer than the originals, but all the necessary sweet-and-salty peanut butter flavor is there, and they'll still send you straight back to your childhood days. Sometimes I like to dip one half of the cookie in melted dark chocolate because I'm extra like that.

TO MAKE THE NUTTER BUTTERS

Adjust the oven rack to the middle position and preheat the oven to 350°F [180°C]. Line two baking sheets with parchment paper or silicone baking mats.

In a medium bowl, whisk together the flour and baking powder. Set aside.

In the bowl of a stand mixer fitted with the paddle attachment, beat the peanut butter, butter, brown sugar, granulated sugar, and vanilla on medium-low speed until smooth, about 2 minutes. Add the flour mixture and mix on low for 30 to 60 seconds, or until the dough comes together. The dough consistency will vary depending on what kind of peanut butter you use. If the dough cannot be rolled easily into a ball, add 1 to 2 tablespoons of milk and mix to combine.

Using your hands, roll 2 to 3 teaspoons of dough into an oblong shape 2 to 2½ in [5 to 6 cm] long (like a large Tootsie Roll). Place the dough rolls about 2 in [5 cm] apart on the prepared baking sheets. Use the tines of a fork to press vertical lines down the length of each piece of dough. Use your fingers to pinch the middle of the oblong shape crosswise into a peanut shell shape. Then use the fork again to make perpendicular lines on each end of the peanut shape, creating the traditional peanut butter cookie crosshatch.

cont.

Bake for 10 to 11 minutes, or until the edges are set. For a crispier cookie, bake for closer to 12 minutes. Let cool on the baking sheets for 10 minutes before using a spatula to transfer the cookies to a wire cooling rack. Let cool completely before adding the filling.

TO ASSEMBLE THE COOKIE SANDWICHES
Line up half of the baked cookies and flip them over so they're flat-side up. Use an offset spatula or spoon to spread 1 to 2 tablespoons of the Peanut Butter Filling on the top of each cookie. Top each with a second cookie, flat-side down, and gently press together. If the filling is soft, place the cookie sandwiches in the refrigerator for 15 to 20 minutes, or until the filling sets.

Store the cookies for up to 3 days tightly covered at room temperature. Once the cookie sandwiches are assembled, they should be stored in the refrigerator, tightly covered, and eaten within 2 days.

S'MORES COOKIES
WITH
TOASTED MARSHMALLOW FILLING

S'MORES COOKIES

⅔ cup [80 g] graham cracker crumbs

1½ cups [190 g] all-purpose flour, spooned and leveled

½ teaspoon baking soda

½ teaspoon fine sea salt

10 tablespoons [145 g] unsalted butter, at room temperature

⅔ cup [130 g] light brown sugar, packed

½ cup [100 g] granulated sugar

2 eggs, at room temperature

1 teaspoon vanilla extract

1 cup [180 g] semisweet chocolate chips (optional)

FOR ASSEMBLY

1 recipe Toasted Marshmallow Filling (page 255)

1 recipe Chocolate Ganache made with milk chocolate (page 245)

A nostalgic ode to summertime s'mores, these cookies are filled to the brim with graham cracker crumbs and come complete with a toasted marshmallow filling–all the flavors of everyone's favorite campfire treat in one irresistible cookie sandwich. If you find milk chocolate too sweet for the ganache, swap with dark or bittersweet chocolate. Whether two or ninety-two, cookie lovers of all ages will love these!

TO MAKE THE COOKIES
Adjust the oven rack to the middle position and preheat the oven to 350°F [180°C]. Line two baking sheets with parchment paper or silicone baking mats.

In a medium bowl, whisk together the graham cracker crumbs, flour, baking soda, and salt. Set aside.

In the bowl of a stand mixer fitted with the paddle attachment, beat the butter, brown sugar, and granulated sugar on medium speed for about 2 minutes. Stop the mixer and scrape down the sides of the bowl. Add the eggs one at a time, and mix on medium speed after each addition until combined. Add the vanilla and the dry ingredients and mix on low speed for about 30 seconds, until the dough comes together. Remove the bowl from the mixer and stir in the chocolate chips, if desired, using a wooden spoon or spatula. Do not overmix.

cont.

Using a 2 tablespoon cookie scoop, scoop 8 cookies onto each prepared baking sheet, about 2 in [5 cm] apart. Bake for 12 to 14 minutes, or until the edges are set and the centers are still soft. Rotate the baking sheets halfway through. Let the cookies cool on the baking sheets for 10 minutes before using a spatula to carefully transfer them to a wire cooling rack to cool completely before adding the filling. Repeat with the remaining dough.

TO ASSEMBLE THE COOKIE SANDWICHES

Flip the baked cookies over so they're flat-side up. Transfer the Toasted Marshmallow Filling to a piping bag. Pipe a heaping tablespoon of the filling onto the flat side of half of the cookies. Use an offset spatula to spread the Chocolate Ganache evenly on the flat underside of the remaining half of the cookies. Place each marshmallow-covered cookie on top of a ganache-covered cookie to form a sandwich and press together gently. Refrigerate to set.

Once the cookie sandwiches are chilled, use a kitchen torch to toast the edges of the marshmallow filling until golden brown, if desired.

Store the s'mores cookies tightly covered at room temperature. Once the cookie sandwiches are assembled with the filling and ganache, they are best enjoyed the same day.

CHOCOLATE SANDWICH COOKIES

(A.K.A. HOMEMADE OREOS)

CHOCOLATE COOKIES

¾ cup [170 g] unsalted butter, at room temperature

¾ cup [150 g] granulated sugar

1 teaspoon vanilla extract

¾ teaspoon kosher salt

1 egg, at room temperature

½ cup [40 g] black cocoa powder, sifted

2 cups plus 2 tablespoons [265 g] all-purpose flour, spooned and leveled

FOR ASSEMBLY

1 recipe Vanilla Bean Filling (page 246, see Note)

A hint of black cocoa (a type of ultra-Dutch-process cocoa) and real vanilla bean make a sophisticated take on everyone's favorite chocolate sandwich cookie. It's an excellent everyday cookie—and an easy way to pack some love into school lunches. Or dress them up for a party by using a scalloped-edge cookie cutter for just the right amount of fancy.

TO MAKE THE COOKIES
In the bowl of a stand mixer fitted with the paddle attachment, cream together the butter and sugar until smooth and creamy. Add the vanilla and salt. Mix on low speed until combined. Stop the mixer and scrape down the sides of the bowl. Add the egg. Mix on medium speed until fully incorporated. Add the cocoa powder and mix on low speed until combined. Add the flour, ½ cup [65 g] at a time, until the dough begins to form a ball around the paddle and pulls away from the sides of the bowl. The dough may seem dry at first, but continue mixing until it comes together.

Transfer the dough to a large piece of parchment paper on your work surface. Top with a second piece of parchment paper. Use a rolling pin to roll the dough between the two layers of parchment. The dough should be ¼ to ½ in [6 to 13 mm] thick.

Carefully slide the parchment paper, with the dough between, onto a large cutting board or baking sheet. Refrigerate for 1 hour.

cont.

Preheat the oven to 350°F [180°C]. Line two baking sheets with parchment paper or silicone baking mats.

Remove the dough from the refrigerator and use a 2 in [5 cm] round cookie cutter to cut circles in the dough. Use a spatula to carefully transfer the cookies to the prepared baking sheets, leaving just 1 in [2.5 cm] between each cookie. The cookies will not spread while baking.

Gather up the scraps of dough and repeat the steps, beginning with rolling the dough between two layers of parchment paper. (If the dough becomes very soft, chill it in the refrigerator for 20 minutes before cutting out the cookie shapes.) Place the baking sheets in the refrigerator for 15 minutes to chill the cookies before baking.

Bake the cookies for 8 to 9 minutes, or until the edges look firm and the centers of the cookies are set.

Remove the cookies from the oven and let cool on the baking sheets for 5 to 10 minutes before using a spatula to carefully transfer the cookies to a wire cooling rack to cool completely.

TO ASSEMBLE THE COOKIE SANDWICHES
Remove the Vanilla Bean Filling from the freezer and use a 2 in [5 cm] round cookie cutter to cut out rounds of filling. Place one round of filling on the flat underside of a cookie and top with a second cookie, flat-side down, and gently press together. Repeat with the remaining cookies and filling.

Store tightly covered in a cool, dry place for up to 4 days. To freeze, wrap the cookies in a layer of plastic wrap and then place in a plastic bag. Defrost at room temperature before serving.

GOURMET GOLDEN OREOS

2½ cups [315 g] all-purpose flour, spooned and leveled

1 teaspoon kosher salt

¾ cup [150 g] granulated sugar

¾ cup [170 g] unsalted butter, at room temperature

1 egg, at room temperature

2 teaspoons vanilla extract

FOR ASSEMBLY

1 recipe Vanilla Bean Filling (page 246, see Note)

This made-from-scratch version of Golden Oreos brings a deliciously simple twist to the everyday classic with a buttery vanilla shortbread base and a speckled vanilla bean filling. It's leaps and bounds above the boxed version. One minute you're saying, "I'll just have one or two" and before you know it, the whole tray is gone.

TO MAKE THE COOKIES
Whisk together the flour and salt in a medium bowl. Set aside.

In the bowl of a stand mixer fitted with the paddle attachment, beat the sugar and butter on medium-low speed for 1 to 2 minutes, or until combined. Add the egg and vanilla and mix until thoroughly combined. Add the flour mixture and mix on low speed until incorporated.

Lay a 12 in [30.5 cm] strip of plastic wrap on your work surface. Transfer the dough to the middle of the plastic wrap. Wrap the dough in the plastic wrap, using the plastic wrap to help press the dough together into a flat disk. Place the tightly wrapped disk of dough in the refrigerator for at least 1 hour.

Adjust the oven rack to the middle position and preheat the oven to 350°F [180°C]. Line two baking sheets with parchment paper or silicone baking mats. Lightly flour your work surface and a rolling pin.

cont.

NOTE

The filling needs to be made in advance and frozen, so plan ahead.

Remove the dough from the refrigerator and roll it out to ¼ in [6 mm] thick. Use a patterned cookie stamp or a 2 in [5 cm] round cookie cutter to cut circles in the dough. Use a spatula to carefully transfer the dough to the prepared baking sheets, leaving 2 in [5 cm] between each cookie. Refrigerate for about 10 minutes, until firm.

Gather any leftover scraps of dough and form another flat disk. Wrap the disk in plastic wrap and place in the refrigerator again until ready to use, at least 15 minutes.

Transfer the sheets of cut-out cookies from the refrigerator straight to the oven and bake for 8 to 9 minutes. Remove from the oven when the edges are just starting to turn golden brown. Cool the cookies on the baking sheets for 5 minutes before using a spatula to carefully transfer them to a wire cooling rack. Let cool completely before adding the filling. Repeat with the remaining dough.

TO ASSEMBLE THE COOKIE SANDWICHES

Remove the Vanilla Bean Filling from the freezer and use the same 2 in [5 cm] round cookie cutter that you used for the cookies to cut out rounds of filling. Place one round of filling on the flat underside of a cookie and top with a second cookie, flat-side down, and gently press together. Repeat with the remaining cookies and filling.

Store tightly covered in a cool, dry place for up to 4 days. To freeze once assembled, wrap the cookies in plastic wrap and then place in a plastic bag. Bring to room temperature before serving.

HOMEMADE MILANOS

HOMEMADE MILANO COOKIES

1½ cups [190 g] all-purpose flour, spooned and leveled

½ teaspoon fine sea salt

1⅓ cups [160 g] confectioners' sugar, sifted

½ cup [113 g] unsalted butter, at room temperature

1 egg plus 2 egg whites, at room temperature

1 teaspoon vanilla extract

FOR ASSEMBLY

1 recipe Chocolate Ganache (page 245), mint or orange variation (optional)

Growing up, milk chocolate Milanos were my favorite store-bought cookie. When I set out to write this book, I knew I had to re-create the magic of those chocolate-filled, buttery-crisp cookies. I'm not going to lie, this recipe is a bit of a messy endeavor, but I promise the results are worth the chocolate stains on your new white T-shirt. If you're a stickler for perfectly uniform cookies, come armed with a ruler.

TO MAKE THE COOKIES
Whisk together the flour and salt in a medium bowl. Set aside.

In the bowl of a stand mixer fitted with the paddle attachment, beat the confectioners' sugar and butter on medium-low speed for about 2 minutes. Stop the mixer and scrape down the sides of the bowl as needed. Add the egg and egg whites and mix on medium-low speed until combined. Mix in the vanilla. Add the flour mixture and mix on low speed for 30 to 60 seconds, or until the dough comes together.

Transfer the dough into a piping bag fitted with a ½ in [13 mm] round tip (or cut a ½ in [13 mm] opening at the end of a piping or zip-top bag).

Line two baking sheets with parchment paper or silicone baking mats. Place a ruler along the edge of the baking sheet to guide you, and pipe about 2 in [5 cm] of dough in a line on a sheet. Continue piping, spacing the cookies about 2 in [5 cm] apart; they will spread as they bake. Don't be afraid to give some pressure when piping the dough. The cookies should be ½ to ¾ in [13 mm to 2 cm] thick.

cont.

Place the baking sheets in the refrigerator for about 15 minutes. This helps prevent the cookies from spreading too much.

While the cookie dough is chilling, adjust the oven rack to the middle position and preheat the oven to 350°F [180°C].

Remove the baking sheets from the refrigerator and put directly in the oven for 10 to 11 minutes, or until the edges of the cookies are slightly golden brown.

Let cool for 10 minutes before using a spatula to carefuly transfer the cookies to a wire cooling rack. Let cool completely before adding the filling.

TO ASSEMBLE THE COOKIE SANDWICHES
Line up half of the baked cookies and flip them over so they're flat-side up. Use an offset spatula to spread some of the Chocolate Ganache on top of each cookie. Top each with a second cookie, flat-side down, and gently press together until the ganache reaches the edges.

Store the cookie sandwiches in an airtight container at room temperature for up to 2 days.

CANDY CANE SHORTBREAD
WITH
PEPPERMINT BUTTERCREAM AND WHITE CHOCOLATE DRIZZLE

CANDY CANE SHORTBREAD

1⅔ cups [210 g] all-purpose flour, spooned and leveled

1 tablespoon cornstarch

1 cup [226 g] unsalted butter, at room temperature

⅔ cup [70 g] sifted confectioners' sugar

1½ teaspoons vanilla extract

½ teaspoon salt

½ cup [80 g] finely crushed candy canes or peppermint candies, plus more for topping

FOR ASSEMBLY

1 recipe Peppermint Buttercream (page 254)

6 oz [170 g] chopped white chocolate

There's no other cookie that looks more festive than these peppermint-studded shortbread sandwiches. Sprinkled with crushed candy canes for added color and crunch, these deserve a standing spot in your holiday cookie box.

TO MAKE THE SHORTBREAD
In a medium bowl, whisk together the flour and cornstarch and set aside.

In the bowl of a stand mixer fitted with the paddle attachment, mix the butter, confectioners' sugar, vanilla, and salt on medium-low speed until light and creamy, about 1 minute. With the mixer on low speed, gradually add the flour mixture. Mix on low speed until the dough comes together but a few streaks of flour remain.

Remove the bowl from the stand mixer and stir in the crushed candy canes with a wooden spoon or spatula. Do not overmix.

Transfer the dough to your work surface and divide it in half. Wrap one half in plastic wrap and set aside. Use a rolling pin to roll out the other half of dough between two large pieces of parchment paper until it is ¼ in [6 mm] thick. (To keep the parchment paper from sliding on the countertop, place it on top of a silicone baking mat.) Repeat with the second half of the dough. Stack the parchment-lined dough slabs one on top of the other on a large baking sheet and refrigerate for 1 hour, or until firm.

cont.

Preheat the oven to 350°F [180°C]. Line two baking sheets with parchment paper or silicone baking mats.

Remove the dough from the refrigerator and peel off the parchment paper. Use a 2 in [5 cm] round cookie or biscuit cutter to cut rounds from each slab of dough. Use a metal spatula to transfer the rounds to the prepared baking sheets. Place the cookies ½ in [13 mm] apart. They will not spread while baking. Gather any scraps of dough and repeat the process, chilling the dough once more if it becomes soft. You should end up with 40 to 44 cookies.

Bake for 9 to 10 minutes. The cookies should be pale but set on the edges. Do not overbake. Allow the cookies to cool on the baking sheet for 5 minutes before using a spatula to carefully transfer the cookies to a wire cooling rack. Let cool completely before assembling the cookie sandwiches.

TO ASSEMBLE THE COOKIE SANDWICHES
Using an offset spatula, spread 1 tablespoon of the Peppermint Buttercream on the flat underside of one cookie. Top with a second cookie, flat-side down, and gently press together, being careful not to smoosh the frosting out the sides. Repeat with the remaining cookies until all the sandwiches are assembled.

Melt the white chocolate in a heatproof bowl in the microwave for 30 seconds. Stir and repeat until smooth and shiny. Carefully transfer the melted white chocolate to a piping bag.

Cut off the very tip of the piping bag and drizzle the tops of the cookies, working quickly before the chocolate hardens.

Sprinkle the top of each cookie sandwich with more crushed candy canes.

Store the assembled cookie sandwiches tightly covered at room temperature for up to 3 days.

SUGAR COOKIES

2¾ cups [345 g] all-purpose flour, spooned and leveled

1½ teaspoons baking powder

½ teaspoon salt

¾ cup [170 g] unsalted butter, at room temperature

2 oz [55 g] full-fat cream cheese, at room temperature

1¼ cups [150 g] confectioners' sugar, sifted

1 egg, at room temperature

1 teaspoon vanilla extract

¼ teaspoon almond extract

Pink food coloring (optional)

FOR ASSEMBLY

1 recipe Vanilla Buttercream (page 246)

Pink food coloring (optional)

SWEETHEART SUGAR COOKIES

Let's be real here. Any cut-out cookie is a bit of a production, but these are about as easy as it gets. And who doesn't love a heart-shaped cookie? Cream cheese is the secret ingredient that makes these sugar cookies super soft and adds a little tang to cut the sweetness of the frosting. I added a drop of pink food coloring to both the cookies and the buttercream, but feel free to tint them whatever color your heart desires.

TO MAKE THE COOKIES

In a medium bowl, whisk together the flour, baking powder, and salt.

In the bowl of a stand mixer fitted with the paddle attachment, beat the butter and cream cheese on medium speed until combined, about 2 minutes. Add the confectioners' sugar and mix on low speed until fully incorporated, then increase the speed to medium and mix for 30 seconds. Stop the mixer and scrape down the sides of the bowl as needed. Add the egg, vanilla, almond extract, and food coloring, if desired. Mix on low speed until fully incorporated. Slowly add the flour mixture and mix on low speed until combined.

Transfer the dough to your work surface and divide it in half. Wrap one half in plastic wrap and set aside. Use a rolling pin to roll the other half of the dough between two large pieces of parchment paper until it is ¼ in [6 mm] thick. (To keep the parchment paper from sliding on the countertop, place it on top of a silicone baking mat.) Repeat with the second half of the dough. Stack the parchment-lined dough slabs one on top of the other on a large baking sheet and refrigerate for 1 hour, or until firm.

cont.

Meanwhile, adjust the oven rack to the middle position and preheat the oven to 350°F [180°C]. Line two baking sheets with parchment paper or silicone baking mats.

Remove the rolled-out dough from the refrigerator and use a 2 to 3 in [5 to 7.5 cm] heart-shaped cookie cutter to cut the dough into shapes. Place the cookies on the prepared baking sheets 1 in [2.5 cm] apart. They will not spread while baking. Bake for 8 to 9 minutes, or until the edges are set. Do not bake until the edges begin to brown or the cookies will be dry.

Remove the cookies from the oven and let cool on the baking sheets for 5 minutes before using a spatula to carefully transfer the cookies to a wire cooling rack to cool completely before adding the buttercream. Repeat with the remaining dough.

TO ASSEMBLE THE COOKIE SANDWICHES
Transfer the Vanilla Buttercream to a piping bag. Pipe about 1½ tablespoons of the frosting onto the flat side of one cookie and top with a second cookie, flat-side down. Repeat with the remaining cookies and frosting.

Store the cookie sandwiches tightly wrapped in the refrigerator for up to 3 days or freeze for up to 2 months. Defrost at room temperature before serving.

CARROT CAKE COOKIES
WITH
BROWN BUTTER
CREAM CHEESE FROSTING

CARROT CAKE COOKIES

1⅔ cups [210 g] all-purpose flour, spooned and leveled

¾ cup [75 g] rolled oats (not steel cut)

1 teaspoon ground cinnamon

¾ teaspoon baking soda

½ teaspoon baking powder

½ teaspoon salt

¼ teaspoon ground nutmeg

¾ cup [150 g] granulated sugar

½ cup [100 g] light brown sugar, packed

½ cup [113 g] unsalted butter, at room temperature

2 eggs, at room temperature

1 teaspoon vanilla extract

1 cup [120 g] finely grated carrot, not packed (about 2 medium carrots)

FOR ASSEMBLY

1 recipe Brown Butter Cream Cheese Frosting (page 257)

Standing at the kitchen counter grating carrots is not my idea of a good time, but I'd happily do it all day long for just one of these carrot cake cookie sandwiches. They're everything you love about carrot cake but in cookie form. That said, if you like raisins in your carrot cake, I'm afraid you'll have to look elsewhere. I can, however, offer you a cream cheese frosting like no other. The brown butter really makes it sing—don't skip it.

TO MAKE THE COOKIES
In a medium bowl, whisk together the flour, oats, cinnamon, baking soda, baking powder, salt, and nutmeg. Set aside.

In the bowl of a stand mixer fitted with the paddle attachment, beat the granulated sugar, brown sugar, and butter on medium-low speed for about 2 minutes. Stop the mixer to scrape down the sides of the bowl as needed. Add the eggs and mix until combined. Mix in the vanilla. Add the flour mixture and mix on low speed for 30 to 60 seconds, or until just combined. Remove the bowl from the mixer and stir in the grated carrot with a wooden spoon or spatula. Cover and chill the dough for at least 3 hours or overnight.

Adjust the oven rack to the middle position and preheat the oven to 350°F [180°C]. Line two baking sheets with parchment paper or silicone baking mats.

Scoop about 2 tablespoons of dough for each cookie onto the prepared baking sheets, leaving 3 inches [7.5 cm] between each cookie. Using your fingers, gently flatten each cookie.

cont.

Bake for 10 to 11 minutes, or until the edges are set but the centers are puffed up. Do not overbake. To help form more uniform, round cookies, use the inside curved part of a fork or a large round cookie cutter to jiggle and even out the edges of the cookies as soon as you pull them from the oven. Let the cookies cool for 10 minutes on the baking sheet before using a spatula to carefully transfer them to a wire cooling rack. Let cool completely before adding the filling.

TO ASSEMBLE THE COOKIE SANDWICHES

Line up half of the baked cookies and flip them over so they're flat-side up. Transfer the Brown Butter Cream Cheese Frosting to a piping bag. Pipe about 2 tablespoons of frosting onto a cookie. Top with a second cookie, flat-side down, and gently press together. Repeat with the remaining cookies until all the sandwiches are assembled.

The cookies will keep for 3 days in an airtight container at room temperature. Once the cookie sandwiches are assembled, they should be stored in the refrigerator and eaten within 2 days.

FOR THE LOVE OF CHOCOLATE

MAKES
12 to 14 cookie sandwiches

WANNABE BROWNIE COOKIES
WITH
PEANUT BUTTER FROSTING

WANNABE BROWNIE COOKIES

½ cup plus 2 tablespoons [80 g] all-purpose flour, spooned and leveled

2 tablespoons Dutch-process cocoa powder

¾ teaspoon baking powder

½ teaspoon salt

7 oz [200 g] good-quality semisweet chocolate, chopped

2 oz [55 g] bittersweet chocolate, chopped

6 tablespoons [85 g] unsalted butter, at room temperature

½ cup [100 g] granulated sugar

¼ cup [50 g] light brown sugar, packed

2 eggs, at room temperature

2 tablespoons freshly brewed espresso or strong coffee, slightly cooled

1½ teaspoons vanilla extract

3 oz [85 g] mini semisweet chocolate chips

Flaky sea salt, for sprinkling (optional)

FOR ASSEMBLY

1 recipe Peanut Butter Frosting (page 256)

These are really just fudgy brownies masquerading as cookies, and they've been breaking hearts and taking names since 2018. One of the very first recipes published on my blog, these uber-chocolatey numbers are perfect for those days when you can't decide between a brownie and a cookie. Add a swirl of fluffy peanut butter frosting, and they are impossible to resist.

TO MAKE THE COOKIES
Preheat the oven to 325°F [165°C]. Line two baking sheets with parchment paper or silicone baking mats.

In a medium bowl, sift together the flour, cocoa powder, baking powder, and salt. Whisk to combine and set aside.

Create a double boiler by filling a medium saucepan with 2 to 3 in [5 to 7.5 cm] of water. Bring the water to a simmer over medium-low heat. Place a heatproof bowl over the pan, making sure that the bottom of the bowl does not touch the water below. Add the semisweet chocolate, bittersweet chocolate, and butter and heat, stirring often. Do not overheat. Once melted, remove the bowl from the heat and stir until the mixture is smooth and shiny. Set aside to cool slightly.

cont.

In the bowl of a stand mixer fitted with the paddle attachment, cream together the granulated sugar, brown sugar, eggs, espresso, and vanilla until thickened, about 2 minutes. Add the chocolate mixture and blend on low speed until combined. Add the flour mixture gradually and mix until barely combined. You should still see some streaks of flour in the batter. The batter will be soft, similar to cake batter.

Remove the bowl from the mixer and gently fold in most of the chocolate chips, reserving 1 to 2 tablespoons for the tops of the cookies if desired. Do not overmix.

Let the dough sit for 5 to 10 minutes at room temperature. Use a 2 tablespoon cookie scoop to portion the cookie dough onto the prepared baking sheets, leaving 2 in [5 cm] between each cookie.

Bake for 8 to 10 minutes, or until the edges are barely set and the centers of the cookies still look soft and fudgy. The cookies will continue to bake a bit once removed from the oven. As soon as the cookies are out of the oven, use the inside arch of a fork to nudge the edges of the cookies in toward the center, working your way around each cookie while they are still hot. This will help make the cookies more uniform in size and shape for the sandwiches.

Allow the cookies to rest for 6 to 8 minutes on the baking sheets before using a spatula to carefully transfer them to a wire cooling rack. Let cool completely before assembling the sandwiches.

TO ASSEMBLE THE COOKIE SANDWICHES

Using an offset spatula, place a generous swirl of the Peanut Butter Frosting on the flat side of a cookie. Top with a second cookie, flat-side down, and gently press together. Repeat with the remaining cookies until all the sandwiches are assembled. If the frosting is soft, place the cookie sandwiches in the refrigerator for 20 minutes to set.

Store tightly covered in the refrigerator for up to 4 days. The Peanut Butter Frosting may soften too much if kept at room temperature.

PEPPERMINT BROWNIE COOKIES
WITH
WHITE CHOCOLATE BUTTERCREAM

PEPPERMINT BROWNIE COOKIES

1 cup [125 g] all-purpose flour, spooned and leveled

¾ cup [95 g] bread flour, spooned and leveled

¼ cup [20 g] Dutch-process cocoa powder

1 teaspoon baking powder

1 teaspoon baking soda

1 teaspoon salt

8 oz [230 g] bittersweet chocolate chips or chopped chocolate

½ cup [113 g] unsalted butter

1 cup [200 g] granulated sugar

½ cup [100 g] light brown sugar, packed

3 eggs, at room temperature

1 teaspoon peppermint extract

FOR ASSEMBLY

1 recipe White Chocolate Buttercream (page 250)

Melted dark chocolate, for topping (optional)

Crushed candy canes, for topping (optional)

Come the end of December, I'm about 95 percent peppermint, thanks in large part to these peppermint brownie cookies. This is my favorite spin on the holiday season's most delicious flavor duo—chocolate and peppermint. I like to make them mini so I can easily lose count of how many I've eaten in a single sitting. These sammies are delicious served straight from the fridge, and I actually prefer them on the second day—if they last that long.

TO MAKE THE COOKIES
In a medium bowl, whisk together the all-purpose flour, bread flour, cocoa powder, baking powder, baking soda, and salt. Set aside.

Create a double boiler by filling a medium saucepan with 2 to 3 in [5 to 7.5 cm] of water. Bring the water to a simmer over medium-low heat. Place a heatproof bowl over the pan, making sure that the bottom of the bowl does not touch the water below. Add the chocolate and butter and heat, stirring often. Do not overheat. Once melted, remove the bowl from the heat and stir until the mixture is smooth and shiny. Pour the melted chocolate mixture into the bowl of a stand mixer fitted with the whisk attachment and allow to cool slightly.

Once the chocolate mixture has cooled slightly, add the granulated sugar, brown sugar, and eggs. Mix on medium-low speed until well combined. Add the peppermint extract and whisk to combine.

cont.

Add the flour mixture to the chocolate mixture and mix until the flour is incorporated. Do not overmix. Cover the bowl with plastic wrap and refrigerate for 30 to 45 minutes.

Once the dough is chilled, preheat the oven to 350°F [180°C]. Line two baking sheets with parchment paper or silicone baking mats.

Use a 2 tablespoon cookie scoop to portion out the cookie dough. For best results, use a kitchen scale to weigh each cookie dough ball so that the cookies are uniform once baked. Regular-size cookies should weigh about 1.3 ounces [39 g]. For mini cookies, use a 2 teaspoon cookie scoop and make cookie dough balls that weigh about 0.8 ounce [24 g]. Roll each cookie dough ball in your hands to create a round ball. Place the balls on the prepared baking sheets, about 2 in [5 cm] apart.

Bake for 9 to 10 minutes, or until the edges are set and the centers of the cookies begin to puff and crack slightly. For mini cookies, bake for 7 to 8 minutes, watching the oven carefully so as not to overbake.

Remove the cookies from the oven and let cool on the baking sheets for 10 minutes before using a spatula to carefully transfer them to a wire cooling rack to cool completely.

TO ASSEMBLE THE COOKIE SANDWICHES
Transfer the White Chocolate Buttercream to a piping bag fitted with a large star tip. Pipe about 1½ tablespoons of buttercream on the flat side of a cookie. Top with a second cookie, flat-side down, and press together gently. Repeat with the remaining cookies and buttercream until all the sandwiches are assembled. If the buttercream is soft, place the cookie sandwiches in the refrigerator until set.

Top the cookies with a drizzle of melted dark chocolate and crushed candy canes, if desired.

Store the cookies tightly covered at room temperature for up to 3 days. They freeze well, tightly covered, for up to 2 months. Defrost at room temperature.

CHOCOLATE PINWHEEL COOKIES
WITH
VANILLA BUTTERCREAM

CHOCOLATE PINWHEEL COOKIES

1 oz [30 g] unsweetened chocolate, melted

1½ cups [190 g] all-purpose flour, spooned and leveled

¾ teaspoon baking powder

¼ teaspoon kosher salt

½ cup plus 1 tablespoon [115 g] granulated sugar

½ cup [113 g] unsalted butter, at room temperature

1 egg, at room temperature

¾ teaspoon vanilla extract

FOR ASSEMBLY

1 recipe Vanilla Buttercream (page 246)

These cookies require a few additional steps, none of which are complicated on their own. But they do involve a handful of extra dishes that will need washing. Bribe your children. Beg your partner. Persuade your roommates. You can pay in fresh-from-the-oven pinwheel cookies— a fair trade if you ask me. I resisted the urge to make this recipe overly decadent, but a dollop of chocolate ganache on top of the vanilla buttercream would give these major bake-me-now vibes.

TO MAKE THE COOKIES

Melt the unsweetened chocolate in the microwave, stirring every 30 seconds until smooth and shiny. Set aside to cool slightly.

In a medium bowl, whisk together the flour, baking powder, and salt. Set aside.

In the bowl of a stand mixer fitted with the paddle attachment, beat the sugar and butter on medium-low speed for about 2 minutes. Stop the mixer and scrape down the sides of the bowl as needed. Add the egg and mix until well combined. Mix in the vanilla. Add the flour mixture and mix on low speed for 30 to 60 seconds, or until the dough comes together. Remove half the dough and mix the melted chocolate into the remaining half in the stand mixer.

Transfer the doughs to separate pieces of plastic wrap. Tightly wrap the doughs in the plastic, making a flat square shape about 1½ in [4 cm] thick. Place the tightly wrapped squares of dough in the refrigerator for at least 2 hours or overnight.

cont.

Once the dough is chilled, lightly flour your work surface and a rolling pin. Place the plain dough on top of the chocolate dough. Roll out the dough in a rectangular shape that is 16 in [40.5 cm] long and 6½ to 7 in [16.5 to 18 cm] wide and about ¼ in [6 mm] thick. The short end of the rectangle should be facing you.

Starting at the bottom of the rectangle (the shorter end that is closest to you), tightly roll the dough up to meet the top. Be careful to roll tightly to avoid any gaps. Gently crimp the seam closed with your hands. Wrap the rolled log of dough in plastic wrap and place in the freezer for 1 hour. (At this point, you can also freeze the dough for up to 2 months.)

While the rolled log of dough is chilling in the freezer, adjust the oven rack to the middle position and preheat the oven to 350°F [180°C]. Line two baking sheets with parchment paper or silicone baking mats.

Remove the log of dough from the freezer and, using a sharp knife, slice ¼ in [6 mm] thick cookies. Slightly rotate the log after each slice to keep the shape consistently round. Place the sliced cookies on the prepared baking sheet and chill in the refrigerator for 15 minutes. If the dough becomes soft and the slices lose their round shape when being cut, place the log back in the freezer for 10 to 15 minutes to firm up.

Bake for 10 to 12 minutes, or until the edges are set and just beginning to brown. Rotate the baking sheets halfway through. Let the cookies cool for 10 minutes on the baking sheet before using a spatula to carefully transfer them to a wire cooling rack. Let cool completely before adding the filling.

TO ASSEMBLE THE COOKIE SANDWICHES
Transfer the Vanilla Buttercream to a piping bag. Pipe about 1½ tablespoons of buttercream onto the flat side of a cookie. Top with another cookie, flat-side down, and gently press together. Repeat with the remaining cookies and buttercream until all the sandwiches are assembled.

Store the cookies for 1 week in an airtight container at room temperature. Once the cookie sandwiches are assembled, they should be stored in the refrigerator and eaten within 2 days.

MOCHA CHOCOLATE WHOOPIE PIES
WITH
SALTED CARAMEL BUTTERCREAM

WHOOPIE PIES

1½ cups [190 g] all-purpose flour, spooned and leveled

⅓ cup [25 g] Dutch-process cocoa powder, sifted

½ teaspoon baking powder

½ teaspoon baking soda

½ teaspoon salt

½ cup [120 ml] buttermilk, at room temperature

1½ tablespoons espresso powder

¾ cup [150 g] light brown sugar, packed

½ cup [120 ml] canola oil

1 egg, at room temperature

1 teaspoon vanilla extract

¼ cup [60 ml] hot water

FOR ASSEMBLY

1 recipe Salted Caramel Buttercream (page 243)

The good news is you won't be able to resist these mini mocha whoopie pies. The bad news is that you won't be able to resist these mini mocha whoopie pies. These little cake-like treats can serve as bookends to any number of frostings and fillings. I'm partial to a swirl of salted caramel buttercream, but peppermint or espresso frosting would be a solid choice. It's worth mentioning that they freeze beautifully and defrost in mere minutes—perfect for midnight snacking.

TO MAKE THE WHOOPIE PIES

Preheat the oven to 350°F [180°C]. Line two baking sheets with parchment paper or silicone baking mats. It's helpful to have a mat with a template for uniform whoopie pies. Alternatively, you can use the bottom of a small measuring cup or glass to draw 2 in [5 cm] circles on the sheets of parchment paper to use as a guide when you pipe the batter.

In a medium bowl, combine the flour, cocoa powder, baking powder, baking soda, and salt. Whisk together and set aside.

In a glass measuring cup, combine the buttermilk and espresso powder. Whisk until the espresso powder dissolves.

cont.

In a large bowl, stir together the brown sugar and oil, mixing to combine well. Add the buttermilk mixture. Stir in the egg and vanilla. Add the dry ingredients and stir gently to combine. Do not overmix. Pour in the hot water and stir until incorporated. The mixture will be somewhat thin, like cake batter.

Transfer the batter to a large piping bag fitted with a large round tip. Carefully pipe 2 in [5 cm] circles onto the prepared baking sheets, leaving 1 in [2.5 cm] between each. You should have 44 to 48 circles total.

Bake for 10 to 12 minutes, or until the whoopie pies spring back when touched and a toothpick inserted into the center comes out clean.

Allow the whoopie pies to cool on the baking sheet for 10 minutes before using a spatula to carefully transfer them to a wire cooling rack to cool completely.

TO ASSEMBLE THE WHOOPIE PIES
Transfer the Salted Caramel Buttercream to a piping bag fitted with a plain round tip. Pipe the buttercream onto the flat side of a whoopie pie. Top with another whoopie pie, flat-side down, and gently press together. Repeat with the remaining whoopie pies and buttercream until all the sandwiches are assembled. Place them in the refrigerator for 30 minutes to allow the buttercream to set.

Store the assembled whoopie pies tightly covered in the refrigerator for up to 4 days. They may be frozen for up to 2 months. To defrost, let sit at room temperature for 20 minutes.

CHOCOLATE COCONUT ALFAJORES

ALFAJORES

1¼ cups [155 g] all-purpose flour, spooned and leveled

½ cup [70 g] cornstarch, spooned and leveled

½ cup [40 g] Dutch-process cocoa powder

½ teaspoon baking powder

¼ teaspoon baking soda

½ teaspoon fine sea salt

1 cup [226 g] unsalted butter, at room temperature (if possible, leave the butter out overnight)

½ cup [100 g] granulated sugar

2 egg yolks, at room temperature

1 teaspoon vanilla extract

FOR ASSEMBLY

1 recipe Dulce de Leche (page 242)

¾ cup [65 g] sweetened finely shredded coconut (optional)

If you've never had a proper alfajor before, the time has come. Originally from Latin America, these bite-size cookies are filled with a creamy dulce de leche and rolled in shredded coconut. They beg to be paired with a cup of strong coffee. The homemade dulce de leche takes about 3 hours to make, so make it ahead of time or prepare it the day before you make the chocolate shortbread.

TO MAKE THE ALFAJORES
In a medium bowl, whisk together the flour, cornstarch, cocoa powder, baking powder, baking soda, and salt. Set aside.

In the bowl of a stand mixer fitted with the paddle attachment, beat the butter and sugar on medium-low speed until pale and creamy, about 3 minutes. Stop the mixer and scrape down the sides of the bowl. Add the egg yolks and vanilla and mix on medium-low speed for another 30 seconds. Add the flour mixture in two additions, mixing on low speed after each addition, until the dough comes together.

Lay a piece of plastic wrap on your work surface and transfer the dough to the middle of the plastic wrap. Tightly wrap the dough in the plastic, forming it into a flat disk about 1½ in [4 cm] thick, and refrigerate for at least 2 hours or overnight.

Line two baking sheets with parchment paper or silicone baking mats. Place in the refrigerator to chill. (You can use one baking sheet repeatedly, but by using two, you won't need to wait for one sheet to completely cool before using it again. It is important to keep the baking sheet and dough on the colder side to help hold the rounded cookie shape.)

cont.

Once the dough is chilled, lightly flour your work surface and a rolling pin. Roll out the dough to ¼ in [6 mm] thick. Use a 2 in [5 cm] round cookie cutter to cut out 40 to 44 circles. Place the cookies, 1 to 2 in [5 to 7.5 cm] apart, on one of the prepared baking sheets and chill in the refrigerator for about 10 minutes.

After you have rolled out the dough for the first time and cut out as many cookies as possible, combine the scraps and form another flat disk about 1½ in [4 cm] thick. Wrap the disk in plastic wrap and refrigerate again for 15 minutes. Continue to roll out the dough and cut the cookie shapes, refrigerating the dough between each round, until all the cookie dough has been used.

While the sheet of cut-out cookies is chilling in the refrigerator, adjust the oven rack to the middle position and preheat the oven to 350°F [180°C].

When the oven is ready, transfer the chilled baking sheet of cookies to the oven and bake for 10 to 12 minutes, or until the edges are set. Remove from the oven and let cool on the baking sheet for 5 minutes before using a spatula to carefully transfer the cookies to a wire cooling rack to cool completely before adding the filling.

TO ASSEMBLE THE COOKIE SANDWICHES
Transfer the Dulce de Leche to a piping bag. Line up half of the baked cookies and flip them over so they are flat-side up. Pipe about ½ tablespoon of Dulce de Leche onto the flat side of each flipped-over cookie. Place the open-faced cookies in the refrigerator for 10 to 15 minutes to firm up the Dulce de Leche (see Note). Once the filling is somewhat firm, remove from the refrigerator and top each with a second cookie, flat-side down, and gently press each sandwich cookie together. Roll the edges of each sandwich cookie in coconut, if desired.

Store the cookies for up to 1 week, tightly sealed in an airtight container. The Dulce de Leche can be kept in a covered jar for 2 to 3 weeks in the refrigerator. Once the cookie sandwiches are assembled, they can be stored at room temperature and should be eaten within 3 days.

COFFEE LOVER'S COOKIES

COFFEE LOVER'S COOKIES

1¼ cups [225 g] semisweet chocolate chips

½ cup [113 g] unsalted butter

¾ cup [95 g] all-purpose flour, spooned and leveled

¼ cup [20 g] Dutch-process cocoa powder, sifted, plus more for dusting

1 teaspoon baking powder

½ teaspoon kosher salt

2 tablespoons instant coffee or espresso powder

⅔ cup [130 g] granulated sugar

½ cup [100 g] light brown sugar, packed

2 eggs, at room temperature

½ teaspoon vanilla extract

Flaky sea salt, for sprinkling (optional)

FOR ASSEMBLY

1 recipe Espresso Buttercream (page 250)

This recipe is adapted from the absurdly delicious Brownie Crinkle Cookies created by Edd Kimber, *The Boy Who Bakes*. In my version, I add a hint of espresso to the dough and an espresso buttercream filling, which together make these sandwich cookies one of life's greatest pleasures. The first time I made them, they were gone before they had even finished cooling. I baked them again the next day and labeled them with a sign that read "don't even think about it" to ward off any lurking cookie monsters.

To get the shiny, crackled tops on the cookies, it is important to measure and prepare all the ingredients in advance so that you can work quickly once you begin. You will also need to bake all the cookies immediately after the dough is made. If you chill the dough, the crinkle top will not look the same after being baked, but the cookies will still taste delicious.

TO MAKE THE COOKIES

Adjust the oven racks so that you can cook two baking sheets at the same time (one rack in the top third of the oven and one in the bottom third of the oven) and preheat the oven to 350°F [180°C]. Line two baking sheets with parchment paper or silicone baking mats.

Create a double boiler by filling a medium saucepan with 2 to 3 in [5 to 7.5 cm] of water. Bring the water to a simmer over medium-low heat. Place a heatproof bowl over the pan, making sure that the bowl does not touch the water below. Add the chocolate chips and butter and cook, stirring often. Do not overheat.

cont.

While the chocolate is melting, in a medium bowl, sift together the flour, cocoa powder, baking powder, and salt. Whisk to combine. Set aside.

When the chocolate and butter are melted and smooth, quickly stir in the instant coffee. Remove the bowl from the heat and set aside to cool slightly. When removing the bowl, be careful not to let any of the steam or water from the saucepan touch the chocolate mixture.

In a large mixing bowl, combine the granulated sugar and brown sugar. Add the eggs and mix with a hand mixer on medium-high speed for 5 minutes. Add the chocolate mixture and the vanilla and mix for 20 to 30 seconds on medium-high speed, or until incorporated. Add the dry ingredients all at once and mix for about 10 seconds, until just combined. Use a sturdy spatula to give the batter a couple more turns to incorporate all the dry ingredients. The batter will be thick like brownie batter.

Using a 2 tablespoon cookie scoop, place about 12 leveled scoops of batter on each of the prepared baking sheets. They will spread slightly in the oven, so allow about 2 in [5 cm] between each cookie.

Place both baking sheets in the oven and bake for 9 to 10 minutes. The tops of the cookies will be crackled and shiny. Do not overbake. Remove from the oven and sprinkle with flaky sea salt, if desired. Let cool on the baking sheet for at least 30 minutes before adding the filling.

TO ASSEMBLE THE COOKIE SANDWICHES
Transfer the Espresso Buttercream to a piping bag fitted with a large tip. Flip half of the cookies over so they're flat-side up. Pipe 2 to 3 tablespoons of filling onto the flat side of the flipped-over cookies. Top each with a second cookie, flat-side down, and gently press together to form a sandwich.

These cookies are best eaten on the day they are made.

HOT FUDGE SUNDAE MACARONS

CHOCOLATE MACARONS

125 g confectioners' sugar

100 g finely ground blanched almond flour

10 g Dutch-process cocoa powder

100 g egg whites, at room temperature (from about 3 eggs)

105 g granulated sugar

Brown gel food coloring, to make the macarons darker (optional)

FOR ASSEMBLY

1 recipe Vanilla Buttercream (page 246)

⅓ cup [80 ml] store-bought hot fudge sauce, at room temperature

¼ cup [45 g] semisweet chocolate chips, melted

3 tablespoons chopped peanuts

This recipe was inspired by one of my favorite desserts: the hot fudge sundae. These rich, chocolatey macarons are filled with a dollop of hot fudge and a swirl of fluffy vanilla buttercream. Top them off with a drizzle of melted chocolate and a sprinkle of crushed peanuts. These fancy French confections are sure to impress!

TO MAKE THE MACARONS

Line two baking sheets with silicone mats printed with macaron templates. Alternatively, line the baking sheets with sheets of parchment paper that have been traced with 1½ in [4 cm] circles spaced 2 in [5 cm] apart. Set aside.

In a large bowl, sift together the confectioners' sugar, almond flour, and cocoa powder through a fine-mesh sieve four times. Discard any large pieces of almond that do not sift through the sieve.

In the bowl of a stand mixer fitted with the whisk attachment, beat the egg whites on medium-high speed until light and foamy, about 1 minute. Slowly add the granulated sugar, 1 tablespoon at a time, while continuing to beat on medium-high speed. Wait 10 to 15 seconds between each addition to be sure the sugar is incorporated. After all the sugar has been added, continue to beat the egg whites on medium-high speed until stiff peaks form. If adding gel food coloring, do so just before mixing is complete so as not to overmix the egg whites. The egg whites should be thick and fluffy and hold their shape when the whisk is turned upright. Continue mixing if the peaks fall over. Be careful not to overmix.

cont.

Once the egg whites hold stiff peaks, add half of the almond flour mixture to the egg whites. Do not stir the mixture but rather fold the ingredients together using broad, sweeping motions with a spatula. Scrape from the bottom of the bowl up and over the top of the mixture. Before incorporating fully, add the remaining dry ingredients and continue the folding motion. Pause to press the batter firmly against the sides of the bowl every now and then to smooth the batter. Continue folding until the batter begins to flow like lava and you can lift the spatula in a figure-8 motion without the mixture breaking off. If it falls off, continue mixing for three or four folds at a time. Test again. The mixture is ready when the ribbon of batter melts back into itself in about 10 seconds. Do not overmix, as your batter will become runny and the macarons will not bake properly.

Scoop the batter into a piping bag or thick plastic bag fitted with a ½ in [13 mm] plain tip. Pipe the macaron batter onto the prepared templates. The circles should measure 1¼ to 1½ in [3 to 4 cm]. When piping, hold the tip perpendicular to the baking sheet and apply pressure to the top of the piping bag to keep a continuous flow of batter through the tip. Release the pressure and use a small flick of the hand to end the flow of batter and leave a smooth top on the macaron. Repeat with the remaining batter. Tap each baking sheet firmly on the countertop three times to release any air bubbles.

Allow the macarons to rest at room temperature for 30 to 60 minutes, or until the tops of the cookies are dry to the touch. (Depending on the weather, this can take over an hour.) Do not skip this step, or the macarons will not bake properly.

Meanwhile, adjust the oven rack to the lower center position and preheat the oven to 325°F [165°C].

Once the macaron tops are dry, place a sheet of macarons in the lower center rack of the preheated oven and bake for 13 to 14 minutes, rotating halfway through the baking time. The macarons are done when the tops are firm and remain attached to the base, or the "feet," when touched. Repeat with the remaining macarons.

Remove the pan from the oven and let cool on the baking sheets for 6 to 8 minutes. Use your hands to gently lift the macarons off the silicone mat and transfer to a wire cooling rack to cool completely.

TO ASSEMBLE THE MACARONS
Transfer the Vanilla Buttercream to a piping bag. Pipe the buttercream in a circle onto the flat side of a macaron, leaving a small hole in the center for the hot fudge. Using a small spoon or another piping bag fitted with a small ¼ in [6 mm] tip, add a dollop of hot fudge in the center of the buttercream. Top with a second macaron, flat-side down, and gently press together just slightly to join the cookies to the buttercream. Repeat with the remaining macarons.

Drizzle the tops of the macarons with melted chocolate and sprinkle with peanuts.

Macarons taste best the day after they are made and will keep in the refrigerator for up to 3 days.

CHEWY CHOCOLATE GINGER COOKIES
WITH
CHOCOLATE GANACHE

CHOCOLATE GINGER COOKIES

2 cups [250 g] all-purpose
flour, spooned and leveled

½ cup [40 g] Dutch-process
cocoa powder

1½ teaspoons baking soda

1 teaspoon ground ginger

1 teaspoon ground cinnamon

½ teaspoon salt

¼ teaspoon ground cloves

¾ cup [170 g] unsalted butter,
at room temperature

½ cup [100 g] granulated
sugar, plus ½ cup [100 g]
for rolling

½ cup [100 g] dark brown
sugar, packed

⅓ cup [105 g] molasses (not
blackstrap)

1 egg, at room temperature

1 teaspoon vanilla extract

FOR ASSEMBLY

1 recipe Chocolate Ganache
(page 245)

This, my friends, is the holiday cookie of my dreams. Baked with Dutch cocoa and a hint of molasses, these cookies are big and chewy and filled with all the warm, cozy gingerbread spices we look forward to the other eleven months of the year. Rolled in sugar and baked to perfection with no chilling time, this twist on the Christmas classic will be a fast favorite among traditional ginger-bread lovers. I could go on and on about how delicious these cookies are, but you really should drop everything and see for yourself.

TO MAKE THE COOKIES
Adjust the oven rack to the middle position and preheat the oven to 325°F [165°C]. Line two baking sheets with parchment paper or silicone baking mats.

In a medium bowl, whisk together the flour, cocoa powder, baking soda, ginger, cinnamon, salt, and cloves. Set aside.

In the bowl of a stand mixer fitted with the paddle attach-ment, beat the butter, ½ cup of granulated sugar, and the brown sugar on medium-high speed until light and creamy, about 3 minutes. Stop the mixer and scrape down the sides of the bowl as needed. Add the molasses and mix on medium-low speed to combine. Stop the mixer and scrape down the sides of the bowl. Add the egg and vanilla and mix until fully incorporated.

Sift the dry ingredients into the butter mixture. Mix on low speed only until incorporated. A few streaks of flour remaining is okay. Do not overmix the dough.

cont.

Remove the bowl from the stand mixer and use a spatula to give the dough one last stir, making sure to scrape down the bottom of the bowl.

Place the remaining ½ cup [100 g] of granulated sugar in a small bowl. Using a 3 tablespoon cookie scoop, scoop the cookie dough and use your hands to shape the dough into a smooth ball. Roll the cookie in the bowl of sugar until all sides are generously covered.

Continue scooping and rolling, placing the cookies on the prepared baking sheets, 3 in [7.5 cm] apart. The cookies will spread as they bake.

Bake for 10 to 11 minutes, or until the cookies have puffed up and have cracks on top. The edges should be set. Do not overbake, or the cookies will be crispy instead of chewy.

Remove the cookies from the oven and let cool on the baking sheet for 10 minutes before using a spatula to care-fully transfer them to a wire cooling rack to cool completely. The cookies will deflate as they cool. Top with a sprinkle of granulated sugar if desired.

TO ASSEMBLE THE COOKIE SANDWICHES
Flip half of the cookies over so they're flat-side up. Spoon about 2 teaspoons of the Chocolate Ganache onto the flat side of the flipped-over cookies. Top each with a second cookie, flat-side down, and gently press together to form a sandwich. Store the cookies for up to 4 days in an airtight container at room temperature. Once the cookie sandwiches are assembled, they should be stored in the refrigerator and eaten within 2 days.

CARAMELIZED WHITE CHOCOLATE COOKIES
WITH
BROWN SUGAR BUTTERCREAM

MAKES
12 cookie sandwiches

CARAMELIZED WHITE CHOCOLATE

8 oz [230 g] pure white chocolate (see Note)

COOKIES

2 cups [250 g] all-purpose flour, spooned and leveled

½ cup [40 g] Dutch-process cocoa powder, sifted

¾ teaspoon baking soda

½ teaspoon instant coffee

½ teaspoon kosher salt

1 cup [226 g] unsalted butter, at room temperature

1 cup [200 g] granulated sugar

½ cup [100 g] light brown sugar, packed

2 eggs, at room temperature

1 teaspoon vanilla extract

Flaky sea salt, for sprinkling (optional)

FOR ASSEMBLY

1 recipe Brown Sugar Buttercream (page 252)

At the risk of sounding super cliché, you haven't lived until you've eaten these cookies. They are a chocolate lover's dream, topped off with one of the greatest creations of our time: caramelized white chocolate. Caramelizing white chocolate is easier than you might think—I'm obsessed! And soon you will be too. All you need is a block of real white chocolate, an oven, a silicone baking mat, and a baking sheet.

TO CARAMELIZE THE WHITE CHOCOLATE
Preheat the oven to 250°F [120°C]. Line a baking sheet with a silicone baking mat. Break the white chocolate into pieces by hand and spread it out on the silicone baking mat. Place in the oven. After 10 minutes, remove from the oven and use an offset spatula to spread the chocolate around.

Repeat this process for a total of 40 to 50 minutes, re-spreading it every 10 minutes. Be sure to move all the chocolate around each time. If it looks lumpy, just keep moving it around with the offset spatula and it will smooth out. The chocolate is done when it darkens to the color of butterscotch or a rich golden brown. Spoon into a glass container and set aside to cool.

It can be covered and kept out on the counter until the cookie dough is ready. Because it's real white chocolate, the caramelized version will firm up and become solid again as it cools. To return it to its liquid state, microwave it in 15-second intervals until melted, or melt it in a heatproof bowl set over a pot of simmering water until smooth.

cont.

NOTE

Make sure the label on the white chocolate reads only "cocoa butter"; it shouldn't contain any other fats or oils. You must use real white chocolate for the caramelization to work. Make the caramelized white chocolate before preparing the cookie dough. Read through the recipe first and allow enough time.

TO MAKE THE COOKIES

Line two baking sheets with parchment paper or silicone baking mats.

In a medium bowl, whisk together the flour, cocoa powder, baking soda, instant coffee, and salt. Set aside.

In the bowl of a stand mixer fitted with the paddle attachment, beat the butter, granulated sugar, and brown sugar on medium-low speed for 1 to 2 minutes, or until creamy. Stop the mixer and scrape down the sides of the bowl. Add the eggs and mix until combined. Add the vanilla and mix to incorporate. Add the flour mixture and mix for about 20 seconds, until just combined. Remove the bowl from the mixer and use a sturdy spatula to give the batter a couple more turns to incorporate all the dry ingredients.

Using a 2 tablespoon cookie scoop, place scoops of dough on one of the lined baking sheets. Chill in the refrigerator for at least 3 hours.

Once chilled, remove the dough balls from the refrigerator and place in the freezer while the oven preheats to 350°F [180°C]. When the oven is ready, remove about ten cookie dough balls from the freezer. Roll each scoop of dough into a ball with your hands, place on the other lined baking sheet, and gently flatten the top. If the caramelized white chocolate has hardened, melt it in the microwave or a double boiler (see page 16) until it is spreadable. Spoon about 2 teaspoons of caramelized white chocolate on top of each cookie dough ball.

Bake the cookies for 9 to 10 minutes, or until the edges are set and the centers are still soft. Do not over bake. Remove from the oven and sprinkle with flaky sea salt, if desired. Let cool on the baking sheet for at least 10 minutes before using a spatula to carefully transfer the cookies to a wire cooling rack. Let cool completely before adding the filling. Repeat with the remaining cookie dough balls.

TO ASSEMBLE THE COOKIE SANDWICHES

Transfer the Brown Sugar Buttercream to a piping bag fitted with a plain round tip. Pipe about 2 tablespoons of buttercream on the flat side of a cookie. Top with a second cookie, flat-side down, and gently press together to form a sandwich. Repeat with the remaining cookies. These cookies are best enjoyed on the day they are made.

CHOCOLATE TRUFFLE COOKIES
WITH
WHIPPED NUTELLA GANACHE

CHOCOLATE TRUFFLE COOKIES

2 cups [250 g] all-purpose flour, spooned and leveled

¾ cup [60 g] Dutch-process cocoa powder

½ teaspoon baking powder

¼ teaspoon salt

1 cup [226 g] unsalted butter, at room temperature

¾ cup [150 g] granulated sugar

1 egg, at room temperature

1 teaspoon vanilla extract

CHOCOLATE COATING

¼ cup [45 g] bittersweet chocolate chips

½ teaspoon coconut oil

FOR ASSEMBLY

1 recipe Whipped Nutella Ganache (page 245)

This cookie sandwich is strictly for true chocolate devotees. I have been obsessed with whipped ganache ever since I frosted a birthday cake with it a few years back. While still rich in flavor, this version of ganache is light as a cloud and made extra decadent with a scoop of hazelnut spread. These cookie sandwiches are nothing short of pure chocolate heaven!

TO MAKE THE COOKIES
In a medium bowl, sift together the flour, cocoa powder, baking powder, and salt. Whisk to combine.

In the bowl of a stand mixer fitted with the paddle attachment, cream together the butter and sugar on medium-high speed until light and fluffy, 1 to 2 minutes. Add the egg and vanilla and mix to combine. Stop the mixer and scrape down the sides of the bowl as needed. Gradually add the flour mixture and mix on low speed until just combined.

Transfer the dough to your work surface and divide it in half. Wrap one half in plastic wrap and set aside. Use a rolling pin to roll the other half of the dough between two large pieces of parchment paper until it is about ¼ in [6 mm] thick. (To keep the parchment paper from sliding on the countertop, place it on top of a silicone baking mat.) Repeat with the second half of the dough. Stack the parchment-lined dough slabs one on top of the other on a baking sheet and refrigerate for 2 hours, until firm.

cont.

Once the dough has chilled, preheat the oven to 350°F [180°C]. Line two baking sheets with parchment paper or silicone baking mats.

Use a 2 in [5 cm] round cookie cutter to cut rounds of dough and transfer them to the prepared baking sheets. Place them 1 in [2.5 cm] apart; the cookies will not spread while baking.

Bake for 10 minutes. Remove from the oven and, using a spatula, carefully transfer the cookies to a wire cooling rack to cool completely.

TO MAKE THE CHOCOLATE COATING

Place the chocolate chips and coconut oil in a microwave-safe bowl. Melt in the microwave in 30-second increments, stirring in between. Continue until the chocolate is smooth and shiny.

Line a baking sheet with parchment or wax paper. Dunk the top of each cookie in the melted chocolate and then transfer to the lined baking sheet to set.

TO ASSEMBLE THE COOKIE SANDWICHES

Once the chocolate coating has set, fill a piping bag fitted with a large star tip with the Whipped Nutella Ganache. Pipe swirls of ganache on the flat side (opposite the chocolate-covered side) of half of the cookies. Top the frosted cookies with the remaining cookies, chocolate-side up. Place in the refrigerator for 30 to 60 minutes to set.

Store the cookies tightly covered in the refrigerator for up to 3 days. Serve cold or let sit out at room temperature for 15 minutes before serving.

BOOZY IRISH CREAM MACARONS

MACARONS

115 g finely ground almond flour

115 g confectioners' sugar

2 tablespoons Dutch-process cocoa powder

2 teaspoons espresso powder (finely ground, not granules)

100 g egg whites (from about 3 eggs)

¼ teaspoon cream of tartar

90 g superfine granulated sugar

FOR ASSEMBLY

1 recipe Bailey's Buttercream (page 254)

Melted white chocolate, for drizzling (optional)

Sprinkles, for decorating (optional)

If you love sipping on Bailey's (the ultimate holiday libation), this will be your new favorite cookie. Made with a hint of espresso and swirls of Irish cream filling, these boozy macarons have some serious personality. The recipe is easy enough for beginners—just follow the directions to a T.

TO MAKE THE MACARONS
Line two baking sheets with silicone mats printed with macaron templates. Alternatively, line the baking sheets with sheets of parchment paper that have been traced with 1½ in [4 cm] circles spaced 2 in [5 cm] apart. Set aside.

In a large bowl, sift together the almond flour, confectioners' sugar, cocoa powder, and espresso powder through a fine-mesh sieve four times. Discard any large pieces of almond that do not sift through the sieve.

In the bowl of a stand mixer fitted with the whisk attachment, mix the egg whites on medium-high speed until light and foamy, about 1 minute. Add the cream of tartar and begin to slowly add the granulated sugar, 1 tablespoon at a time, while continuing to whisk on medium-high speed. Wait 10 to 15 seconds between each addition to be sure the sugar is incorporated. After all the sugar has been added, continue to beat the egg whites on medium-high speed until stiff peaks form. The egg whites should be thick and fluffy and hold their shape when the whisk is turned upright. Continue mixing if the peaks fall over. Be careful not to overmix.

cont.

Once the egg whites hold stiff peaks, add half of the almond flour mixture to the egg whites and use a spatula to fold together. Do not stir the mixture but rather fold the ingredients together using broad, sweeping motions. Scrape from the bottom of the bowl and up and over the top of the mixture. Before incorporating fully, add the remaining dry ingredients and continue the folding motion. Pause to press the batter firmly against the sides of the bowl every now and then to smooth the batter.

Continue folding until the batter begins to flow like lava and you can lift the spatula in a figure-8 motion without the mixture breaking off. If it falls off, continue mixing for three or four folds at a time. Test again. The mixture is ready when the ribbon of batter melts back into itself in about 10 seconds. Do not overmix, as your batter will become runny and the macarons will not bake properly.

Scoop the batter into a piping bag or thick plastic bag fitted with a ½ in [13 mm] plain tip. Pipe the macaron batter onto the prepared templates. Circles should measure 1¼ to 1½ in [3 to 4 cm]. When piping, hold the tip perpendicular to the baking sheet and apply pressure to the top of the piping bag to keep a continuous flow of batter through the tip. Release the pressure and use a small flick of the hand to end the flow of batter and leave a smooth top on the macaron. Repeat with the remaining batter. Tap each baking sheet firmly on the countertop three times to release any air bubbles.

Allow the macarons to rest at room temperature for 30 to 60 minutes, or until the tops of the cookies are dry to the touch. (Depending on the weather, this can take over an hour.) Do not skip this step or the macarons will not bake properly.

Meanwhile, adjust the oven rack to the lower center position and preheat the oven to 325°F [165°C].

Once the macaron tops are dry, place a single sheet of macarons in the oven and bake for 13 minutes. The macarons are done when the tops are firm and remain attached to the base, or "feet," when touched. Repeat with the remaining macarons.

cont.

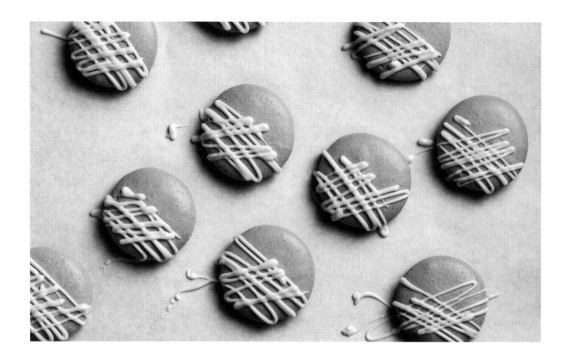

Remove the pan from the oven and let cool completely on the silicone mats for 6 to 8 minutes. Use your hands to gently lift the macarons off of the silicone mat and transfer to a wire cooling rack to cool completely.

TO ASSEMBLE THE MACARONS

Transfer the Bailey's Buttercream to a piping bag. Pipe a small swirl of buttercream onto the flat side of a macaron. Top with a second macaron, flat-side down, and very gently press the two together to seal. Repeat with the remaining cookies and buttercream. If desired, drizzle the melted white chocolate over the macarons and top with sprinkles. Place in the refrigerator to set.

Macarons are best stored tightly covered in the refrigerator and taste best the day after they are made.

DOUBLE MINT CHOCOLATE COOKIE SANDWICHES

CHOCOLATE MINT COOKIES

1¾ cups [220 g] all-purpose flour, spooned and leveled

¾ cup [60 g] Dutch-process cocoa powder, sifted

½ teaspoon salt

1 cup [226 g] unsalted butter, at room temperature

¾ cup [150 g] granulated sugar

1 egg white, at room temperature

1 teaspoon vanilla extract

½ teaspoon peppermint extract

CHOCOLATE COATING

12 oz [340 g] semisweet or bittersweet chopped chocolate

½ teaspoon canola oil

FOR ASSEMBLY

1 recipe Mint Chocolate Ganache (page 245)

Flaky sea salt, for sprinkling (optional)

These mini minty sandwiches have *late night snack* written all over them. With a chocolate cookie, ganache, and coating, this recipe takes full advantage of the fact that you can never have too much chocolate. All that's missing is a tall glass of cold milk. Enjoy them cold straight from the freezer.

TO MAKE THE COOKIES
In a medium bowl, combine the flour, cocoa powder, and salt. Whisk together and set aside.

In the bowl of a stand mixer fitted with the paddle attachment, cream together the butter and sugar on medium-high speed until light and creamy. Add the egg white, vanilla, and peppermint extract and mix to combine. Stop the mixer and scrape down the sides of the bowl. Add the flour mixture in two batches, mixing on low speed until just combined.

Remove the bowl from the mixer and use a sturdy spatula to give one more stir to ensure all the flour is incorporated.

Transfer the dough to your work surface and divide it in half. Wrap one half in plastic wrap and set aside. Use a rolling pin to roll the other half of the dough between two large pieces of parchment paper until it is about ¼ in [6 mm] thick. (To keep the parchment from sliding on the countertop, place it on top of a silicone baking mat.) Repeat with the second half of the dough. Stack the parchment-lined dough slabs one on top of the other on a baking sheet. Refrigerate for 1½ to 2 hours, or until firm.

cont.

Preheat the oven to 350°F [180°C]. Line another baking sheet with parchment paper or a silicone baking mat.

Remove the dough from the refrigerator and use a 1½ to 2 in [4 to 5 cm] cookie cutter to cut small rounds of dough, placing them on the prepared baking sheet, ½ in [13 mm] apart (the cookies will not spread while baking). Gather the scraps of the dough and continue to roll it out between two pieces of parchment paper until all the dough is used. If the dough becomes soft as you work, place the cut-out cookies in the refrigerator for 20 minutes before baking. (This is a good time to make the Mint Chocolate Ganache, as it needs to rest for about 30 minutes before using.)

Bake for 8 to 10 minutes, or until the edges are set. Bake 1 to 2 minutes longer for crispier cookies. Remove the cookies from the oven and let cool on the baking sheet for 5 minutes before using a spatula to carefully transfer the cookies to a wire cooling rack to cool completely.

TO MAKE THE CHOCOLATE COATING
Melt the chocolate and canola oil together over a double-boiler or using the microwave. (Adding a splash of oil to the chocolate keeps it from seizing and makes it easier to dunk the cookies.) Stir until melted and smooth. Set aside to cool for about 5 minutes.

TO ASSEMBLE THE COOKIE SANDWICHES
Line a baking sheet with parchment or wax paper.

Use a teaspoon or offset spatula to spread about 1 teaspoon of the Mint Chocolate Ganache on the flat side of a cookie. Top with a second cookie, flat-side down. Rest the cookie sandwich on a large fork and dip it into the chocolate coating, being sure to cover all sides of the cookie. Lift the fork up and allow the excess chocolate to drip back into the bowl. Repeat with the remaining cookies, ganache, and chocolate coating.

Place the finished cookie sandwiches on the prepared baking sheet, sprinkle with flaky salt, if desired, then let cool. Refrigerate to speed this along.

Store the cookies tightly covered in the refrigerator for up to 1 week or freeze for up to 3 months.

THE COOL COOKIES

CHOCOLATE CHIP COOKIE ICE CREAM SANDWICHES

(LIKE A CHIPWICH, BUT BETTER)

CHOCOLATE CHIP COOKIES

2¾ cups [345 g] all-purpose flour, spooned and leveled

1 teaspoon cornstarch

1 teaspoon baking soda

1 teaspoon salt

1 cup [226 g] unsalted butter, cubed and cold

¾ cup [150 g] light brown sugar, packed

⅔ cup [130 g] granulated sugar

1 egg plus 1 egg yolk, at room temperature

1 tablespoon vanilla extract

2¼ cups [405 g] semisweet chocolate chips

FOR ASSEMBLY

¾ cup [135 g] mini semisweet chocolate chips, for rolling (optional)

1 recipe Slow-Churn Vanilla Ice Cream (page 262), or 1½ qt [1.4 L] store-bought vanilla ice cream (see Note)

Step aside, Chipwich. This homemade version of everyone's favorite ice cream sandwich pays homage to the original with a giant, brown-sugary chocolate chip cookie stuffed with made-from-scratch vanilla ice cream and rolled in a coating of mini chocolate chips. There is no part of this cookie sandwich that doesn't make me extremely happy—it's pure childhood nostalgia and far superior to anything store-bought. Trust me.

TO MAKE THE COOKIES
Preheat the oven to 375°F [190°C]. Line two baking sheets with parchment paper or silicone baking mats.

In a medium bowl, whisk together the flour, cornstarch, baking soda, and salt. Set aside.

In the bowl of a stand mixer fitted with the paddle attachment, beat together the butter, brown sugar, and granulated sugar for 3 to 4 minutes, or until pale and fluffy. Stop the mixer and scrape down the sides of the bowl. Add the egg and egg yolk, one at a time, stopping to scrape down the sides of the bowl between each addition. Mix in the vanilla. Add the flour mixture and mix on low speed until well combined.

Remove the bowl from the mixer and stir in the chocolate chips with a wooden spoon or sturdy spatula. Do not overmix.

Use a 3 tablespoon cookie scoop to scoop the cookies onto the prepared baking sheets, leaving 2 to 3 in [5 to 7.5 cm] between each cookie.

cont.

Bake for 9 to 11 minutes, or until the edges are browned and the centers are light and puffy. Halfway through baking, remove each pan from the oven and firmly tap it on the countertop twice to help flatten the cookies. Rotate the pan and continue baking. Once the edges of the cookies are set and the centers are slightly puffed up, remove the cookies from the oven. Tap the baking sheet firmly on the countertop twice more. Let cool on the baking sheet for 10 minutes before using a spatula to carefully transfer the cookies to a wire cooling rack to cool completely.

TO ASSEMBLE THE ICE CREAM SANDWICHES
Freeze the cooled cookies for 20 to 30 minutes, until firm. Place the mini chocolate chips in a shallow bowl or plate. Use a round cookie cutter the same size as the cookies to cut rounds of frozen vanilla ice cream from the pan. Place an ice cream round on the flat side of a chocolate chip cookie. Top with a second cookie, flat-side down, and press gently together to seal.

Quickly roll the outside edges of the cookie sandwich in the mini chocolate chips. Immediately place the cookie sandwich in the freezer to set. Repeat with the remaining cookies, ice cream, and mini chocolate chips. Freeze for at least 2 hours, or for best results, overnight.

Store the cookies (without ice cream) in an airtight container for up to 4 days. Once the ice cream sandwiches are assembled, keep tightly wrapped in the freezer for up to 2 months.

COOKIE DOUGH ICE CREAM BROWNIE SANDWICHES

EDIBLE CHOCOLATE CHIP COOKIE DOUGH

4 tablespoons [55 g] unsalted butter, at room temperature

¼ cup [50 g] light brown sugar, packed

3 tablespoons granulated sugar

1 tablespoon heavy cream or whole milk

¼ teaspoon vanilla extract

½ cup plus 2 tablespoons [80 g] heat-treated all-purpose flour (see Notes)

Pinch of kosher salt

½ cup [90 g] mini semisweet chocolate chips

ICE CREAM FILLING

1 recipe Slow-Churn Vanilla Ice Cream (page 262), or 1½ qt [1.4 L] store-bought vanilla ice cream (see Notes)

BROWNIES

1 cup [226 g] salted butter

7 oz [200 g] bittersweet chocolate chips

2 tablespoons Dutch-process cocoa powder, sifted

2 teaspoons vanilla extract

3 eggs, at room temperature

1⅓ cups [265 g] granulated sugar

1 cup [125 g] all-purpose flour, spooned and leveled

To call these ice cream sandwiches a bit over the top would be accurate. The hardest part is not eating all the edible cookie dough before it makes its way into the ice cream. If you make it past that part, the rest is a piece of cake.

Prepare the cookie dough ice cream a day or two ahead to break up the workload and allow time for it to freeze.

TO MAKE THE EDIBLE COOKIE DOUGH

In a medium bowl, use an electric hand mixer to cream together the butter, brown sugar, and granulated sugar. Beat on medium-high speed for 2 minutes. Add the heavy cream and vanilla and mix for 1 minute. Add the heat-treated flour and salt and mix to combine well. Use a spatula or wooden spoon to stir in the mini chocolate chips.

Turn the dough out onto a large piece of plastic wrap and form it into a rectangle about 1½ in [4 cm] thick. Wrap in the plastic and refrigerate for 1 hour.

TO MAKE THE ICE CREAM FILLING

Once the cookie dough is chilled, cut it into bite-size pieces and stir into the prepared (or softened store-bought) vanilla ice cream. Spread the cookie dough ice cream into a 9 by 13 in [23 by 33 cm] baking pan and freeze overnight.

TO MAKE THE BROWNIES

Preheat the oven to 325°F [165°C]. Line a 9 by 13 in [23 by 33 cm] baking pan with parchment paper, allowing the ends of the paper to extend over the sides of the pan by 1 to 2 in [2.5 to 5 cm] for easy removal of the brownies once cool.

cont.

Typically flour is baked into a recipe, but in edible cookie dough, the flour remains raw. Raw flour can carry harmful bacteria. Heat-treating the flour makes it safe to use in any no-bake dessert.

To heat-treat the flour, place 1 cup [125 g] of flour on a clean, dry baking sheet and bake at 350°F [180°C] for 5 minutes. Remove from the oven and cool completely before measuring out the amount needed for the recipe.

If using store-bought ice cream, prepare it ahead of time: Soften the ice cream at room temperature and use a large spatula to spread it into a parchment-lined 9 by 13 in [23 by 33 cm] baking pan. Use an offset spatula to level the top, working quickly so that the ice cream doesn't melt completely. Freeze overnight.

In a medium saucepan over medium-high heat, melt the butter, stirring occasionally.

Once the butter has melted, carefully pour it into a heat-proof bowl. Immediately stir in the chocolate chips, cocoa powder, and vanilla. Stir until the chocolate is completely melted and the mixture is shiny. Set aside to cool for 10 minutes.

In the bowl of a stand mixer fitted with the whisk attachment, beat together the eggs and granulated sugar on medium speed until light and creamy, about 3 minutes.

Once the chocolate mixture has cooled, slowly pour it into the egg mixture and continue to beat on medium speed for about 30 seconds. Remove the bowl from the mixer and stir in the flour by hand with a silicone spatula or wooden spoon. Do not overmix.

Pour the batter into the prepared pan and use an offset spatula to spread the batter toward all four corners of the pan. Bake for 20 to 22 minutes, or until the edges of the brownies are set and the center no longer looks underbaked.

Remove the pan from the oven and allow to cool completely before cutting. To remove the brownies from the pan, pull up on the parchment paper overhang and set the brownies on your work surface. Using a sharp knife, trim the edges of the brownies and then cut the brownies into even rectangles about 4½ by 2½ in [11 by 6 cm].

TO ASSEMBLE THE ICE CREAM SANDWICHES

Cut the cookie dough ice cream into same-size rectangles as the brownies. Use a knife or offset spatula to transfer an ice cream cutout onto the bottom side of a cooled brownie. Top with a second brownie, bottom-side down, and press together gently to form a sandwich. Repeat with the remaining brownies and ice cream.

Immediately place the ice cream sandwiches in the freezer to set for a minimum of 2 hours. For best results, freeze overnight.

Store the brownies (without ice cream) in an airtight container for up to 4 days. Once the ice cream sandwiches are assembled, keep tightly wrapped in the freezer for up to 2 months.

BLACK COCOA BROWNIE MINT CHIP SANDWICHES

BLACK COCOA BROWNIES

1 cup [180 g] bittersweet chocolate chips

½ cup [113 g] unsalted butter

⅓ cup [25 g] black cocoa powder, sifted

¾ cup [150 g] granulated sugar

½ cup [100 g] light brown sugar, packed

2 eggs, at room temperature

2 teaspoons vanilla extract

¾ cup [95 g] all-purpose flour, spooned and leveled

¼ teaspoon salt

FOR ASSEMBLY

1 recipe Mint Chip Ice Cream (page 263), or 1½ qt [1.4 L] store-bought mint chip ice cream (see Note)

Black cocoa is a close cousin of Dutch cocoa and the darkest of all the cocoa powders. If you've never used black cocoa powder before, let this recipe be the reason you give it a go. These brownies bake up decadently dark, fudgy, and extremely chocolatey—all good things in my book. The best part is the batter comes together in just minutes in one pot on the stove top—ideal for those days you can't be bothered to break out the mixer. I like to cut them in bite-size squares so I don't feel bad about going back for seconds and thirds.

TO MAKE THE BROWNIES

Preheat the oven to 350°F [180°C]. Line a 9 by 13 in [23 by 33 cm] baking pan with parchment paper. Allow the edges of the parchment to extend over the sides of the pan by 1 to 2 in [2.5 to 5 cm] for easy removal of the brownies once baked. Set aside.

In a medium pot over medium-low heat, melt the chocolate chips and butter. Stir occasionally until fully melted and smooth.

Remove the pot from the heat and stir in the cocoa powder. Whisk together until well combined. Let the mixture sit for 5 minutes. Add the granulated sugar and brown sugar to the pot and whisk the mixture for 2 full minutes. Add the eggs one at a time until fully incorporated. Stir in the vanilla. Mix in the flour and salt. Leave a few streaks of flour remaining. Do not overmix.

Transfer the batter to the prepared pan and use a spatula to spread it evenly, pressing the batter into the corners of the pan. It will be thin.

cont.

NOTE

If using store-bought ice
cream, prepare it ahead of
time: Soften the ice cream at
room temperature and use a
large spatula to spread it into
a parchment-lined 9 by 13 in
[23 by 33 cm] baking pan. Use
an offset spatula to level the
top, working quickly so that
the ice cream doesn't melt
completely. Freeze overnight.

Bake for 16 to 18 minutes, or until the edges are set. Remove
the pan from the oven and let the brownies cool in the pan
for 10 minutes. Use the parchment paper overhang to lift the
brownies out of the pan and transfer to a wire cooling rack
to cool completely.

TO ASSEMBLE THE ICE CREAM SANDWICHES

Trim the edges of the brownies and then use a square
cookie cutter or sharp knife to cut 3 in [7.5 cm] squares.
Use the same cookie cutter to cut squares of the mint chip
ice cream. Place a square of ice cream on the flat side of
a brownie and then top with a second brownie, flat-side
down. Gently press together to form a sandwich. Repeat
with the remaining brownies and ice cream.

Immediately place the brownie ice cream sandwiches in
the freezer for 2 hours or, for best results, overnight.

Store the brownies (without ice cream) in an airtight container for up to 4 days. Once the ice cream sandwiches
are assembled, keep tightly wrapped in the freezer for up
to 2 months.

BLACK FOREST ICE CREAM SANDWICHES

CHOCOLATE COOKIES

2 cups [250 g] all-purpose flour, spooned and leveled

⅔ cup [50 g] Dutch-process cocoa powder

2 teaspoons cornstarch

¾ teaspoon baking powder

½ teaspoon espresso powder

½ teaspoon salt

1 cup plus 2 tablespoons [230 g] granulated sugar

¾ cup [170 g] unsalted butter, at room temperature

1 egg, at room temperature

1 teaspoon vanilla extract

FOR ASSEMBLY

1 recipe Cherry Ice Cream (page 263), or 1½ qt [1.4 L] store-bought cherry ice cream (see Note)

I love cherries! Fresh, frozen. In a jam or baked in a pie. Chocolate-covered or à la mode. Come summer, all I can think about are these Black Forest Ice Cream Sandwiches. These frozen sammies will make you lots of friends at the neighborhood pool party. Don't dillydally—cherry season doesn't last long.

TO MAKE THE COOKIES
In a medium bowl, sift together the flour, cocoa powder, cornstarch, baking powder, espresso powder, and salt. Whisk to combine and set aside.

In the bowl of a stand mixer fitted with the paddle attachment, cream together the sugar and butter on medium-high speed until light and fluffy, about 3 minutes. Stop the mixer and scrape down the sides of the bowl. Add the egg and vanilla and mix to combine. Gradually add the flour mixture and mix on low speed until a soft dough forms. Do not overmix.

Transfer the dough to a large piece of parchment paper and pat it into a flat rectangular shape about 1 in [2.5 cm] thick. Place on a baking sheet and cover with plastic wrap. Chill the dough for 1 hour in the refrigerator.

Adjust the oven rack to the middle position and preheat the oven to 350°F [180°C]. Line two baking sheets with parchment paper or silicone baking mats.

cont.

NOTE

If using store-bought ice cream, prepare it ahead of time: Soften the ice cream at room temperature and use a large spatula to spread it into a parchment-lined 9 by 13 in [23 by 33 cm] baking pan. Use an offset spatula to level the top, working quickly so that the ice cream doesn't melt completely. Freeze overnight.

Remove the dough from the refrigerator, discard the plastic wrap, and place the dough (still on the parchment paper) on your work surface. Add another sheet of parchment paper on top and, using a rolling pin, roll the dough out between the parchment paper until it is ¼ in [6 mm] thick. Work quickly so the dough stays cold.

Use a 2 to 3 in [5 to 7.5 cm] round cookie or biscuit cutter to cut circles in the dough. Use a metal spatula to transfer the cut-outs to one of the prepared baking sheets, placing them about 1 in [2.5 cm] apart.

Immediately place the cookies in the oven and bake for 12 minutes. The tops of the cookies should be set but still soft. Let the cookies cool on the baking sheet for 10 minutes before using a spatula to carefully transfer the cookies to a wire cooling rack to cool completely.

Keep any unbaked dough in the refrigerator while each pan of cookies bakes. Repeat by rolling out the scraps of dough until all the cookies are baked. You should end up with 24 to 28 cookies.

For best results, freeze the cookies for 30 minutes before assembling the ice cream sandwiches.

TO ASSEMBLE THE ICE CREAM SANDWICHES
Use a cookie or biscuit cutter the same size as the cookies to cut rounds of the cherry ice cream. Carefully place the ice cream on the flat side of one cookie and top with a second cookie, flat-side down. Gently press together to form a sandwich. Repeat with the remaining cookies and ice cream. Immediately place the sandwiches in the freezer for at least 2 hours or overnight.

Store the cookies (without ice cream) in an airtight container for up to 4 days. Once the ice cream sandwiches are assembled, keep tightly wrapped in the freezer for up to 2 months.

CHOCOLATE-DIPPED PEANUT BUTTER COOKIE ICE CREAM SANDWICHES

PEANUT BUTTER COOKIES

1½ cups [190 g] gluten-free flour, spooned and leveled (see Notes)

1 teaspoon xanthan gum (see Notes)

1 teaspoon baking soda

¼ teaspoon kosher salt

1 cup [200 g] light brown sugar, packed

⅔ cup [170 g] creamy peanut butter, at room temperature

½ cup [113 g] unsalted butter, at room temperature

1 egg, at room temperature

1½ teaspoons vanilla extract

FOR ASSEMBLY

1 recipe Slow-Churn Vanilla Ice Cream (page 262), or 1½ qt [1.4 L] store-bought vanilla ice cream (see Notes)

CHOCOLATE COATING

2 cups [360 g] semisweet chocolate chips

¼ cup [60 g] coconut oil

Scoops of creamy vanilla ice cream sandwiched between two soft-baked peanut butter cookies dunked in a bath of melted dark chocolate. What could be better? I'll wait while you ponder.

TO MAKE THE COOKIES
In a medium bowl, whisk together the flour, xanthan gum, baking soda, and salt. Set aside.

In the bowl of a stand mixer fitted with the paddle attachment, cream together the brown sugar, peanut butter, and butter until light and fluffy, about 3 minutes. Add the egg and vanilla and mix until well combined. Stop the mixer and scrape down the sides of the bowl with a spatula. Add the flour mixture, mixing on low speed until barely combined.

Remove the bowl from the mixer and refrigerate the dough for 3 hours or overnight.

Once the dough is chilled, preheat the oven to 350°F [180°C]. Line two baking sheets with parchment paper or silicone baking mats.

Using a 2 tablespoon cookie scoop, scoop the dough onto the prepared baking sheets, leaving 2 in [5 cm] between each cookie.

cont.

If using a gluten-free flour blend that contains xanthan gum, omit the additional xanthan gum.

If you prefer gluten-full cookies, swap the 1½ cups [190 g] gluten-free flour for 1½ cups [190 g] all-purpose flour, and omit the xanthan gum.

If using store-bought ice cream, prepare it ahead of time: Soften the ice cream at room temperature and use a large spatula to spread it into a parchment-lined 9 by 13 in [23 by 33 cm] baking pan. Use an offset spatula to level the top, working quickly so that the ice cream doesn't melt completely. Freeze overnight.

Bake for 11 to 12 minutes, or until the edges are barely golden brown but the centers are still soft. The cookies will continue to bake as they cool. To make the cookies more uniform in size, use a 3 to 4 in [7.5 to 10 cm] round cookie cutter to "swirl" around the outside edges of each cookie. Do this immediately after removing the cookies from the oven while they are still hot.

Let cool on the baking sheet for 10 minutes before using a spatula to carefully transfer the cookies to a wire cooling rack to cool completely. Freeze the cookies for 30 to 45 minutes before adding ice cream.

TO ASSEMBLE THE ICE CREAM SANDWICHES

Use a cookie cutter the same size as the cookies to cut out rounds of vanilla ice cream. Place an ice cream round on the flat side of one cookie and top with a second cookie, flat-side down. Gently press together to form a sandwich. Repeat with the remaining cookies and ice cream. Freeze for at least 1 hour.

TO MAKE THE CHOCOLATE COATING

Melt the chocolate and coconut oil in a heatproof bowl in the microwave in 30-second intervals, stirring in between each interval, until melted and smooth. Let cool to room temperature.

Line a baking sheet with wax paper.

Carefully dunk one half of each frozen ice cream sandwich in the melted chocolate coating and allow the excess chocolate to drip into the bowl. If possible, hold the sandwich for about 10 seconds so the chocolate begins to set before placing it on the prepared baking sheet. Work quickly to dunk the sandwiches one at a time, returning them to the freezer immediately. For best results, freeze for 2 hours before serving, or overnight.

Store the cookies (without ice cream) in an airtight container for up to 4 days. Once the ice cream sandwiches are assembled, keep tightly wrapped in the freezer for up to 2 months.

PEANUT BUTTER PRETZEL COOKIES
WITH
CHOCOLATE ICE CREAM

PEANUT BUTTER PRETZEL COOKIES

2¼ cups [280 g] all-purpose flour, spooned and leveled

1 teaspoon baking soda

1 teaspoon baking powder

¼ teaspoon ground cinnamon

¼ teaspoon kosher salt

1 cup [226 g] unsalted butter, at room temperature

1 cup [200 g] dark brown sugar, packed

¾ cup [150 g] granulated sugar

⅔ cup [170 g] creamy peanut butter, at room temperature

1 egg, at room temperature

2 teaspoons vanilla extract

1¼ cups [175 g] chopped semisweet or dark chocolate, plus more for tops

1 cup [30 g] mini pretzel twists, chopped into pieces, plus more for tops

FOR ASSEMBLY

1 recipe Classic Chocolate Ice Cream (page 263), or 1½ qt [1.4 L] store-bought chocolate ice cream (see Note)

I hate to play favorites with my recipes, but these might just be the best cookies to ever come out of my oven. There is no better match for peanut butter than chocolate; throw in some pretzels and—O.M.G. These salty-sweet cookies bake up impossibly delicious with puddles of melted chocolate and crunchy pretzel bits. Unless you want to eat them all by yourself, I suggest you invite some people over to share them with you.

TO MAKE THE COOKIES
In a medium bowl, whisk together the flour, baking soda, baking powder, cinnamon, and salt. Set aside.

In the bowl of a stand mixer fitted with the paddle attachment, cream together the butter, brown sugar, and granulated sugar on medium-high speed for 3 minutes, until light and fluffy. Add the peanut butter and mix together for 1 minute until well incorporated. Add the egg and vanilla. Mix to combine. Add the flour mixture in two batches and mix on low speed until just combined. A few streaks of flour remaining is fine.

Remove the bowl from the mixer and use a sturdy spatula or wooden spoon to stir in the chopped chocolate and pretzel pieces.

cont.

NOTE

If using store-bought ice cream, prepare it ahead of time: Soften the ice cream at room temperature and use a large spatula to spread it into a parchment-lined 9 by 13 in [23 by 33 cm] baking pan. Use an offset spatula to level the top, working quickly so that the ice cream doesn't melt completely. Freeze overnight.

Line a baking sheet with parchment paper and use a large 3 tablespoon cookie scoop to scoop the dough onto the baking sheet. The scoops can be side by side on the baking sheet while they chill. Once all the dough has been scooped, add more chunks of chopped chocolate and pretzel bits to the tops, if desired. Chill the dough for 2 hours.

Once the dough has chilled, preheat the oven to 350°F [180°C]. Line two baking sheets with parchment paper or silicone baking mats. Transfer the chilled dough to the prepared baking sheets, spacing the scoops about 2 in [5 cm] apart.

Bake for 12 to 13 minutes, or until the edges of the cookies just begin to brown and the centers of the cookies are puffy. Do not overbake.

Remove the cookies from the oven and let cool on the baking sheet for 10 minutes before using a spatula to carefully transfer the cookies to a wire cooling rack. Let cool completely before assembling the ice cream sandwiches.

TO ASSEMBLE THE ICE CREAM SANDWICHES
Use a cookie cutter the same size as the cookies to cut out rounds of chocolate ice cream from the pan. Place a round of ice cream on the flat side of one cookie and top with a second cookie, flat-side down. Gently press together to form a sandwich. Repeat with the remaining cookies and ice cream. Place the sandwiches in the freezer for a minimum of 2 hours or overnight.

Store the cookies (without ice cream) in an airtight container for up to 4 days. Once the ice cream sandwiches are assembled, keep tightly wrapped in the freezer for up to 2 months.

BROWN SUGAR SCOTCHIES
WITH
CINNAMON ICE CREAM

BROWN SUGAR SCOTCHIES

2¼ cups [225 g] rolled oats (not steel cut)

1¾ cups [220 g] all-purpose flour, spooned and leveled

1 teaspoon baking soda

¾ teaspoon fine sea salt

¼ teaspoon ground cinnamon

1 cup [226 g] unsalted butter, at room temperature

¾ cup [150 g] granulated sugar

½ cup [100 g] light brown sugar, packed

2 eggs, at room temperature

1½ teaspoons vanilla extract

1 cup [160 g] butterscotch chips

1 cup [180 g] chocolate chips

FOR ASSEMBLY

1 recipe Cinnamon Ice Cream (page 263), or 1½ qt [1.4 L] store-bought cinnamon ice cream (see Note)

For those who agree that raisins have no place in oatmeal cookies, you are my people! Throw in a handful of chocolate and butterscotch chips instead and seal the deal with a scoop of cinnamon ice cream. These bake up soft and chewy and will stay that way even when frozen, which makes them especially ideal for sandwich smooshing.

TO MAKE THE COOKIES
Adjust the oven rack to the middle position and preheat the oven to 350°F [180°C]. Line two baking sheets with parchment paper or silicone baking mats.

Add the oats to a food processor fitted with the blade attachment and pulse four or five times, until they are at least halved in size.

Transfer the processed oats to a medium bowl and add the flour, baking soda, salt, and cinnamon. Whisk together to combine and set aside.

In the bowl of a stand mixer fitted with the paddle attachment, beat the butter, granulated sugar, and brown sugar on medium-low for 1 to 2 minutes. Stop the mixer and scrape down the sides of the bowl as needed. Add the eggs, one at a time, mixing until combined. Add the vanilla and mix to combine. Add the dry ingredients and mix on low speed for about 30 seconds, until the dough comes together. Stop the mixer and remove the bowl from the mixer. Add the butterscotch and chocolate chips and gently stir them in with a spatula or wooden spoon.

cont.

NOTE

If using store-bought ice cream, prepare it ahead of time: Soften the ice cream at room temperature and use a large spatula to spread it into a parchment-lined 9 by 13 in [23 by 33 cm] baking pan. Use an offset spatula to level the top, working quickly so that the ice cream doesn't melt completely. Freeze overnight.

Use a 2 tablespoon cookie scoop to portion out the dough and roll each scoop into a ball with your hands. Place onto the prepared baking sheets, leaving 3 in [7.5 cm] between each cookie. Then, using the bottom of a measuring cup (or your hand), gently flatten each cookie dough ball.

Bake for 11 to 12 minutes, or until the edges start to turn golden. Let cool for at least 5 minutes on the pan before using a spatula to carefully transfer the cookies to a wire cooling rack. Let cool completely before assembling the ice cream sandwiches.

TO ASSEMBLE THE ICE CREAM SANDWICHES
Use a cookie cutter the same size as the cookies to cut out rounds of cinnamon ice cream from the pan. Place an ice cream round on the flat side of one cookie and top with a second cookie, flat-side down. Gently press together to form a sandwich. Repeat with the remaining cookies and ice cream. Place the sandwiches in the freezer for a minimum of 2 hours or overnight.

Store the cookies (without ice cream) in an airtight container for up to 4 days. Once the ice cream sandwiches are assembled, keep tightly wrapped in the freezer for up to 2 months.

BROWN BUTTER GINGER COOKIES
WITH
CINNAMON ICE CREAM

BROWN BUTTER GINGER COOKIES

¾ cup [170 g] unsalted butter

1½ cups [190 g] all-purpose flour, spooned and leveled

¾ cup [95 g] bread flour, spooned and leveled

2 teaspoons ground ginger

1½ teaspoons baking soda

1 teaspoon ground cinnamon

½ teaspoon kosher salt

¼ teaspoon ground cloves

¼ teaspoon ground allspice

¾ cup [150 g] dark brown sugar, packed

½ cup [100 g] granulated sugar

1 egg, at room temperature

3 tablespoons molasses (not blackstrap)

1 teaspoon vanilla extract

FOR ASSEMBLY

1 recipe Cinnamon Ice Cream (page 263), or 1½ qt [1.4 L] store-bought cinnamon ice cream (see Note)

At its core, this is a recipe for a simple ginger cookie. Adding brown butter, a bit of molasses, and a scoop of bread flour for extra "chew" elevates it to something special. I wouldn't be mad if you added a splash of bourbon to the dough. Don't knock it till you try it!

TO MAKE THE COOKIES
In a medium saucepan over medium-high heat, melt ½ cup [113 g] of the butter, stirring occasionally. Once the butter begins to crackle and pop, stir continuously. After about 5 minutes, the butter will form a layer of foam over the top and the crackling will stop. Continue to stir the butter as it browns. Amber-brown butter solids will begin to collect on the bottom of the pan. The butter will smell slightly nutty and aromatic and be amber in color.

Remove from the heat and pour the butter into a heat-proof bowl, making sure to scrape all the brown butter solids from the bottom of the pan. Chill in the refrigerator until firm, about 1 hour.

Once the butter has reached a solid state, remove it and the remaining ¼ cup [57 g] of butter from the refrigerator and bring them to room temperature on the counter for about 30 minutes.

Preheat the oven to 350°F [180°C] and line two baking sheets with parchment paper or silicone baking mats.

In a medium bowl, whisk together the all-purpose flour, bread flour, ginger, baking soda, cinnamon, salt, cloves, and allspice. Set aside.

cont.

NOTE

If using store-bought ice cream, prepare it ahead of time: Soften the ice cream at room temperature and use a large spatula to spread it into a parchment-lined 9 by 13 in [23 by 33 cm] baking pan. Use an offset spatula to level the top, working quickly so that the ice cream doesn't melt completely. Freeze overnight.

In the bowl of a stand mixer fitted with the paddle attachment, combine the brown butter and softened butter, the brown sugar, and ¼ cup [50 g] of the granulated sugar. Beat on medium-high speed for 3 minutes, until light and fluffy. Stop the mixer and scrape down the sides of the bowl. Add the egg, molasses, and vanilla. Mix on medium speed until well combined. Stop and scrape down the sides of the bowl once more. Add the flour mixture and mix on low speed until combined, stopping when a few streaks of flour remain.

Remove the bowl from the stand mixer and use a sturdy spatula to give the dough another stir, being sure to run the spatula along the bottom of the bowl.

Place the remaining ¼ cup [50 g] of granulated sugar in a shallow bowl.

Use your hands to form 2 tablespoon–size rounds of dough. Roll the dough between your palms until smooth. Drop each cookie dough ball into the bowl of sugar and toss to coat completely.

Transfer the cookies to the prepared baking sheets, leaving 2 in [5 cm] between each. Bake for 10 to 12 minutes, or until the edges are set and the cookies begin to crack.

Remove the cookies from the oven and let them cool on the baking sheet for 5 to 10 minutes before using a spatula to carefully transfer the cookies to a wire cooling rack to cool completely before adding ice cream.

TO ASSEMBLE THE ICE CREAM SANDWICHES

Use a cookie cutter the same size as the cookies to cut out rounds of frozen cinnamon ice cream. Place a round of ice cream on the flat side of one cookie and top with a second cookie, flat-side down. Gently press together to form a sandwich. Repeat with the remaining cookies and ice cream. Place the sandwiches in the freezer for a minimum of 2 hours or overnight.

Store the cookies (without ice cream) in an airtight container for up to 4 days. Once the ice cream sandwiches are assembled, keep tightly wrapped in the freezer for up to 2 months.

BROWN BUTTER MACADAMIA NUT BLONDIES
WITH
COCONUT ICE CREAM

BLONDIES

⅔ cup [90 g] macadamia nuts

1 cup [226 g] unsalted butter

1¼ cups [250 g] dark brown sugar, packed

2 eggs, at room temperature

1 tablespoon vanilla extract

1¾ cups [220 g] all-purpose flour, spooned and leveled

1 teaspoon baking powder

¼ teaspoon kosher salt

FOR ASSEMBLY

1 recipe Coconut Ice Cream (page 263), or 1½ qt [1.4 L] store-bought coconut ice cream (see Note)

Shredded sweetened coconut, for garnish (optional)

These rich, buttery macadamia nut blondies stuffed with creamy coconut ice cream will transport you straight to the tropics without even boarding a plane. Though technically not a cookie, they're delicious, and a fitting option for those who don't have the time (or patience) to roll and cut cookie dough. Don't hold back on the amount of vanilla called for here. Think of it as a flavor all its own. It's much harder to overdo than one might think.

TO MAKE THE BLONDIES
Grease a 9 by 13 in [23 by 33 cm] baking pan, line it with parchment paper, and lightly grease the parchment as well.

In the bowl of a food processor fitted with the blade attachment, chop the macadamia nuts into small pieces. Transfer the chopped nuts to a small skillet over low heat and toast until toasted and fragrant. Remove from the heat and set aside to cool.

In a medium saucepan over medium-high heat, melt the butter, stirring occasionally. When the butter begins to crackle and pop, begin to stir continuously. After about 5 minutes, the butter will form a layer of foam over the top and the crackling will stop. Continue to stir the butter as it browns. Amber-brown butter solids will collect on the bottom of the pan, and the butter will smell slightly nutty and be amber in color. Remove the pan from the heat and pour the butter into the bowl of a stand mixer fitted with the paddle attachment, scraping the solids from the bottom of the pan. Allow the browned butter to cool for 15 to 20 minutes.

cont.

If using store-bought ice cream, prepare it ahead of time: Soften the ice cream at room temperature and use a large spatula to spread it into a parchment-lined 9 by 13 in [23 by 33 cm] baking pan. Use an offset spatula to level the top, working quickly so that the ice cream doesn't melt completely. Freeze overnight.

Meanwhile, preheat the oven to 350°F [180°C].

Add the brown sugar to the cooled butter in the mixer bowl. Beat on medium speed until the sugar is dissolved. Add the eggs, one at a time, followed by the vanilla. Mix to combine.

In a medium bowl, whisk together the flour, baking powder, and salt.

Remove the bowl from the stand mixer and use a spatula or wooden spoon to stir in the flour mixture. Fold in the toasted macadamias, being careful not to overmix.

Pour the batter into the prepared pan and use a spatula to push the mixture into the corners and level the top. The batter will just cover the bottom of the pan.

Bake for 16 to 18 minutes, or until the edges of the blondies are set and the top is golden brown. The center will still look underbaked, but the blondies will continue to bake as they cool.

Let cool completely before using a 2½ in [6 cm] square cookie or biscuit cutter to cut shapes from the pan. For best results, place the blondie squares on a clean baking sheet in the freezer for 20 to 30 minutes before assembling the ice cream sandwiches.

TO ASSEMBLE THE ICE CREAM SANDWICHES
Use the same cookie cutter used for the blondies to cut squares of coconut ice cream from the pan. Place a square of ice cream on the flat side of a blondie square, top with another blondie square, flat-side down, and gently press together to form a sandwich. Repeat with the remaining blondies and ice cream. Freeze for a minimum of 2 hours or overnight. Before serving, sprinkle the tops with shredded coconut, if desired.

Store the blondies (without ice cream) in an airtight container for up to 4 days. Once the ice cream sandwiches are assembled, keep tightly wrapped in the freezer for up to 2 months.

MOLASSES COOKIES
WITH
BOURBON ICE CREAM

MOLASSES COOKIES

4¼ cups [530 g] all-purpose flour, spooned and leveled

4 teaspoons ground ginger

1 tablespoon baking soda

1 tablespoon ground cinnamon

1½ teaspoons ground cloves

½ teaspoon salt

¾ cup [135 g] shortening

½ cup [120 ml] vegetable or canola oil

1 cup [200 g] dark brown sugar, packed

¾ cup [150 g] granulated sugar

½ cup [160 g] molasses (not blackstrap)

2 eggs, at room temperature

FOR ASSEMBLY

1 recipe Bourbon Ice Cream (page 263), or 1½ qt [1.4 L] store-bought bourbon ice cream (see Note)

My love for molasses runs deep. Come holiday season, I put it in everything from cookies and cakes to pies and tarts. Loaded with heaps of warm, cozy spices, these molasses cookies are rolled in a coating of sugar for extra texture and crunch. For the ultimate finish, I opted for a generous scoop of bourbon-spiked ice cream, although a swirl of eggnog buttercream would be extra festive. You do you!

TO MAKE THE COOKIES

In a medium bowl, whisk together the flour, ginger, baking soda, cinnamon, cloves, and salt until well combined. Set aside.

In the bowl of a stand mixer fitted with the paddle attachment, combine the shortening, vegetable oil, brown sugar, and ½ cup [100 g] of the granulated sugar. Beat on medium speed for 2 to 3 minutes until well combined. Stop the mixer and scrape down the sides of the bowl. Add the molasses and mix on low speed until incorporated. Mix in the eggs, one at a time, until well combined. Stop and scrape down the sides of the bowl after each addition. With the mixer on low speed, gradually add the flour mixture 1 cup [125 g] at a time until combined. Stop the mixer when a few streaks of flour remain.

Remove the bowl from the stand mixer and use a sturdy spatula to fold the batter together until well combined, being careful not to overmix.

Cover the bowl with plastic wrap and refrigerate for 30 minutes.

cont.

NOTE

If using store-bought ice cream, prepare it ahead of time: Soften the ice cream at room temperature and use a large spatula to spread it into a parchment-lined 9 by 13 in [23 by 33 cm] baking pan. Use an offset spatula to level the top, working quickly so that the ice cream doesn't melt completely. Freeze overnight.

While the dough chills, preheat the oven to 350°F [180°C]. Line two baking sheets with parchment paper or silicone baking mats. Place the remaining ¼ cup [50 g] of granulated sugar in a small bowl.

After 30 minutes, remove the dough from the refrigerator and use a 3 tablespoon cookie scoop to scoop the dough into balls. Roll the balls in the granulated sugar to cover on all sides. Place the cookie dough balls 2 in [5 cm] apart on the prepared baking sheets.

Bake for 11 to 12 minutes, or until the edges of the cookies are set and the centers are puffed up. Do not overbake. The cookies will continue to bake as they cool.

Remove the cookies from the oven and allow to cool on the baking sheets for 10 minutes before using a spatula to carefully transfer them to a wire cooling rack to cool completely. For best results, freeze for 30 minutes before assembling the ice cream sandwiches.

TO ASSEMBLE THE ICE CREAM SANDWICHES
Use a cookie or biscuit cutter the same size as the cookies to cut rounds of the bourbon ice cream. Carefully place the ice cream on the flat side of one cookie and top with a second cookie, flat-side down. Gently press together to form a sandwich. Repeat with the remaining cookies and ice cream. Immediately place the sandwiches in the freezer for at least 2 hours or overnight.

Store the cookies (without ice cream) in an airtight container for up to 4 days. Once the ice cream sandwiches are assembled, keep tightly wrapped in the freezer for up to 2 months.

SUGAR COOKIE CONFETTI ICE CREAM SANDWICHES

SUGAR COOKIES

1 cup [226 g] unsalted butter, at room temperature

½ cup [100 g] granulated sugar

½ cup [100 g] light brown sugar, packed

1 egg, at room temperature

2 teaspoons vanilla extract

¼ teaspoon almond extract

3¼ cups [405 g] all-purpose flour, spooned and leveled

¼ teaspoon kosher salt

FOR ASSEMBLY

1 recipe Confetti Ice Cream (page 263), or see Note

Sprinkles, for coating (optional)

I always say, when the going gets tough, just add sprinkles. Consider these sprinkle-topped ice cream sandwiches a surefire mood lifter. If you can manage not to eat all the buttery sugar cookies before you even get to the ice cream, you'll find these frozen treats hard to beat!

TO MAKE THE COOKIES

In the bowl of a stand mixer fitted with the paddle attachment, cream together the butter, granulated sugar, and brown sugar until light and fluffy, about 3 minutes. Stop the mixer and scrape down the sides of the bowl. Add the egg, vanilla, and almond extract and mix for 1 minute more. Add the flour and salt and mix on low speed until combined. The dough should begin to pull away from the sides of the mixing bowl. Do not overmix. A few streaks of flour remaining is okay.

Transfer the dough to your work surface and divide it in half. Wrap one half in plastic wrap and set aside. Use a rolling pin to roll the other half of the dough between two large pieces of parchment paper until it is ¼ in [6 mm] thick. (To keep the parchment from sliding on the countertop, place it on top of a silicone baking mat.) Repeat with the second half of the dough. Stack the parchment-covered dough slabs one on top of the other on a large baking sheet and refrigerate for 1 hour, or until firm.

Meanwhile, adjust the oven rack to the middle position and preheat the oven to 350°F [180°C]. Line two baking sheets with parchment paper or silicone baking mats.

cont.

NOTE

You can easily make Confetti Ice Cream using 1½ qt [1.4 L] store-bought vanilla ice cream. Soften the ice cream at room temperature. Add ½ to ¾ cup [80 to 120 g] rainbow sprinkles to the softened ice cream and stir with a wooden spoon to evenly distribute the sprinkles. Use a large spatula to spread the ice cream into a parchment-lined 9 by 13 in [23 by 33 cm] baking pan. Use an offset spatula to level the top, working quickly so that the ice cream doesn't melt completely. Freeze overnight.

Remove one sheet of rolled-out dough from the refrigerator and use a 3 in [7.5 cm] round cookie cutter to cut the dough into rounds. Place the cookies on the prepared baking sheets 1 in [2.5 cm] apart. Bake for 8 to 10 minutes or until the edges are set and just beginning to turn golden brown. Do not overbake.

Remove the cookies from the oven and allow the cookies to cool on the baking sheets for 5 minutes before using a spatula to carefully transfer the cookies to a wire cooling rack to cool completely. Repeat with the remaining dough. For best results, freeze for 30 minutes before assembling the ice cream sandwiches.

TO ASSEMBLE THE ICE CREAM SANDWICHES
Use the same cookie cutter used for the cookies to cut the confetti ice cream the same size as the cookies. Carefully place the ice cream on the flat side of one cookie and top with a second cookie, flat-side down. Gently press together to form a sandwich. Add more sprinkles to the ice cream edges, if desired, and immediately place in the freezer for at least 2 hours or overnight. Repeat with the remaining cookies and ice cream.

Store the cookies (without ice cream) in an airtight container for up to 4 days. Once the ice cream sandwiches are assembled, keep tightly wrapped in the freezer for up to 2 months.

BANANA SPLIT ICE CREAM SANDWICHES

BANANA COOKIES

2 cups [250 g] all-purpose flour, spooned and leveled

1 teaspoon ground cinnamon

¾ teaspoon baking soda

½ teaspoon salt

½ cup [113 g] unsalted butter, at room temperature

½ cup [100 g] dark brown sugar, packed

⅔ cup [130 g] granulated sugar

1 large banana, mashed

1 egg yolk, at room temperature

1½ teaspoons vanilla extract

FOR ASSEMBLY

1 recipe Chocolate Ganache (page 245), chilled

1 recipe Chocolate Chip Ice Cream (page 263), or 1½ qt [1.4 L] store-bought chocolate chip ice cream (see Note)

½ cup [70 g] chopped nuts, such as peanuts, almonds, or walnuts (optional)

This recipe takes your usual banana split components—bananas, ice cream, chocolate, and nuts—and reimagines them as an irresistible handheld frozen dessert. They're perfect for summer parties and great for feeding a crowd, especially because you can make them in advance. Don't forget the cherry on top!

TO MAKE THE COOKIES
Preheat the oven to 350°F [180°C]. Line two baking sheets with parchment paper or silicone baking mats. In a medium bowl, whisk together the flour, cinnamon, baking soda, and salt. Set aside.

In the bowl of a stand mixer fitted with the paddle attachment, combine the butter, brown sugar, and granulated sugar. Beat on medium-high speed until pale and fluffy, about 3 minutes. Add the banana, egg yolk, and vanilla. Mix for 1 minute to combine well. Stop the mixer and scrape down the sides of the bowl as needed. Add the flour mixture in two additions and mix only until a few streaks of flour remain.

Use a 2 tablespoon cookie scoop to scoop the dough onto the prepared baking sheets. Leave 2 in [5 cm] between each cookie.

Bake for 9 to 10 minutes, or until the edges of the cookies are slightly golden brown.

Remove the pans from the oven and let the cookies cool on the baking sheets for 5 minutes before using a spatula to carefully transfer to a wire cooling rack. Let cool completely before assembling the ice cream sandwiches.

cont.

NOTE

If using store-bought ice
cream, prepare it ahead of
time: Soften the ice cream at
room temperature and use a
large spatula to spread it into
a parchment-lined 9 by 13 in
[23 by 33 cm] baking pan. Use
an offset spatula to level the
top, working quickly so that
the ice cream doesn't melt
completely. Freeze overnight.

TO ASSEMBLE THE ICE CREAM SANDWICHES

Flip over half of the cookies on a baking sheet. Spread about 1 tablespoon of chilled Chocolate Ganache on each of the flipped-over cookies. Place the baking sheet with the cookies in the freezer for 15 minutes.

Use a round cookie cutter the same size as the cookies to cut rounds of chocolate chip ice cream from the pan. Place one of the ice cream rounds on top of the ganache and top with a second cookie, flat-side down. Gently press together to form a sandwich. Repeat with the remaining cookies and ice cream.

Roll the edges of the ice cream sandwiches in the chopped nuts, if desired.

Immediately place the ice cream sandwiches in the freezer to set. Freeze for at least 2 hours or for best results, overnight.

Store the cookies (without ice cream) in an airtight container for up to 4 days. Once the ice cream sandwiches are assembled, keep tightly wrapped in the freezer for up to 2 months.

SEVEN-LAYER BAR COOKIES
WITH
VANILLA ICE CREAM

SEVEN-LAYER BAR COOKIES

1 cup [125 g] all-purpose flour, spooned and leveled

½ cup [60 g] graham cracker crumbs

½ teaspoon baking powder

½ teaspoon baking soda

½ teaspoon kosher salt

½ cup [113 g] unsalted butter, melted and slightly cooled

½ cup [100 g] light brown sugar, packed

⅓ cup [65 g] granulated sugar

1 egg, at room temperature

1½ teaspoons vanilla extract

½ cup [90 g] semisweet chocolate chips

½ cup [80 g] butterscotch chips

½ cup [43 g] sweetened shredded coconut

¼ cup [30 g] walnuts, chopped and lightly toasted

FOR ASSEMBLY

1 recipe Slow-Churn Vanilla Ice Cream (page 262), or 1½ qt [1.4 L] store-bought vanilla ice cream (see Note)

This is one of the last recipes I created for the book, and honestly, I can't believe I didn't come up with it sooner! If you don't have graham crackers and butterscotch chips stocked in your pantry, this is one of those rare times I'm going to ask you to run to the store and get some. I for one will be making these cookie sandwiches on repeat because I feel like I have to make up for lost time!

TO MAKE THE SEVEN-LAYER BARS
Preheat the oven to 350°F [180°C]. Line two baking sheets with parchment paper or silicone baking mats.

In a medium bowl, whisk together the flour, graham cracker crumbs, baking powder, baking soda, and salt. Set aside.

Add the cooled melted butter, brown sugar, and granulated sugar to a large bowl and use a hand mixer to beat together on medium-high speed for about 3 minutes. The mixture will thicken and lighten in color. Add the egg and vanilla and mix until smooth and combined. Add the flour mixture and beat on low speed until just combined. Do not overmix.

Use a spatula or wooden spoon to stir in the chocolate chips, butterscotch chips, coconut, and walnuts.

Use a 2 tablespoon cookie scoop to scoop balls of cookie dough onto the prepared baking sheets. The cookies will spread, so leave 2 to 3 in [5 to 7.5 cm] between each cookie.

cont.

NOTE

If using store-bought ice cream, prepare it ahead of time: Soften the ice cream at room temperature and use a large spatula to spread it into a parchment-lined 9 by 13 in [23 by 33 cm] baking pan. Use an offset spatula to level the top, working quickly so that the ice cream doesn't melt completely. Freeze overnight.

Bake for 10 to 11 minutes, or until the edges of the cookies are set and the centers are still puffy. Remove from the oven and let cool on the baking sheets for 10 minutes before using a spatula to carefully transfer the cookies to a wire cooling rack to cool completely.

TO ASSEMBLE THE ICE CREAM SANDWICHES
Use a cookie cutter the same size as the cookies to cut out rounds of frozen vanilla ice cream. Place a round of the ice cream on the flat side of one cookie and top with a second cookie, flat-side down. Gently press together to form a sandwich. Repeat with the remaining cookies and ice cream. Place the sandwiches in the freezer for a minimum of 2 hours or overnight.

Store the cookies (without ice cream) in an airtight container for up to 4 days. Once the ice cream sandwiches are assembled, keep tightly wrapped in the freezer for up to 2 months.

BROWN BUTTER TOFFEE WALNUT COOKIES
WITH
BOURBON ICE CREAM

BROWN BUTTER TOFFEE WALNUT COOKIES

2 cups [250 g] all-purpose flour, spooned and leveled

2 tablespoons cornstarch

1 teaspoon baking soda

1 teaspoon baking powder

½ teaspoon kosher salt

1 cup [226 g] unsalted butter

1 cup [200 g] dark brown sugar, packed

¾ cup [150 g] granulated sugar

1 egg, at room temperature

2 teaspoons vanilla extract

1 cup [180 g] semisweet chocolate chips

¾ cup [90 g] chopped walnuts, lightly toasted

½ cup [80 g] chocolate-covered toffee bits (such as Skor or Heath)

FOR ASSEMBLY

1 recipe Bourbon Ice Cream (page 263), or 1½ qt [1.4 L] store-bought bourbon ice cream (see Note)

The title alone says it all. Nutty, chewy, chocolatey, these cookies hit every craving and then some. The brown butter cookie dough base is filled with crunchy bits of toffee and walnuts and finished off with pools of melted chocolate. The cookies on their own would be an instant winner at any blue ribbon bake-off or school bake sale, but stuff them with bourbon-spiked ice cream for an adult-only treat you'll want to keep all to yourself.

TO MAKE THE COOKIES
In a medium bowl, whisk together the flour, cornstarch, baking soda, baking powder, and salt. Set aside.

In a medium saucepan over medium-high heat, melt the butter, stirring occasionally. When the butter begins to crackle and pop, begin to stir continuously. After about 5 minutes, the butter will form a layer of foam over the top and the crackling will stop. Continue to stir the butter as it browns. Amber-brown butter solids will collect on the bottom of the pan and the butter will smell slightly nutty and be amber in color.

Remove from the heat and pour into a heatproof bowl, making sure to scrape all the brown butter solids from the bottom of the pan. Chill in the refrigerator until firm. This takes about 1 hour.

cont.

NOTE

If using store-bought ice cream, prepare it ahead of time: Soften the ice cream at room temperature and use a large spatula to spread it into a parchment-lined 9 by 13 in [23 by 33 cm] baking pan. Use an offset spatula to level the top, working quickly so that the ice cream doesn't melt completely. Freeze overnight.

Preheat the oven to 350°F [180°C]. Line two baking sheets with parchment paper or silicone baking mats. Transfer the chilled brown butter to the bowl of a stand mixer fitted with the paddle attachment. Add the brown sugar and granulated sugar and mix on medium-high speed for 3 minutes. The mixture should be light and fluffy. Add the egg and vanilla and mix to combine well. Add the flour mixture and mix on low speed until only a few streaks of flour remain.

Remove the bowl from the stand mixer and add the chocolate chips, chopped walnuts, and toffee bits. Use a spatula or wooden spoon to combine.

Use a 3 tablespoon cookie scoop to scoop the dough onto the prepared baking sheets. Leave at least 2 in [5 cm] between each cookie, as they will spread slightly in the oven. Bake for 10 to 12 minutes, or until the edges of the cookies look set and begin to turn golden brown. The centers of the cookies will look slightly underbaked, but the cookies will continue to bake as they cool.

Remove the cookies from the oven and let cool on the baking sheet for 10 minutes before using a spatula to carefully transfer the cookies to a wire cooling rack to cool completely.

TO ASSEMBLE THE ICE CREAM SANDWICHES
Use a cookie cutter the same size as the cookies to cut out rounds of frozen bourbon ice cream. Place a round of the ice cream on the flat side of one cookie and top with a second cookie, flat-side down. Gently press together to form a sandwich. Repeat with the remaining cookies and ice cream. Place the sandwiches in the freezer for a minimum of 2 hours or overnight.

Store the cookies (without ice cream) in an airtight container for up to 4 days. Once the ice cream sandwiches are assembled, keep tightly wrapped in the freezer for up to 2 months.

INSIDE-OUT WHITE CHOCOLATE CHIP ICE CREAM SANDWICHES

INSIDE-OUT WHITE CHOCOLATE CHIP COOKIES

1 cup plus 2 tablespoons [140 g] all-purpose flour, spooned and leveled

½ cup [40 g] Dutch-process cocoa powder, sifted

1 teaspoon baking soda

½ teaspoon baking powder

½ teaspoon salt

½ cup [113 g] unsalted butter, at room temperature

¾ cup [150 g] light brown sugar, packed

¼ cup [50 g] granulated sugar

1 egg, at room temperature

2 teaspoons vanilla extract

¾ cup [105 g] bittersweet chocolate chunks

⅔ cup [120 g] white chocolate chips

FOR ASSEMBLY

1 recipe Chocolate Chip Ice Cream (page 263), or 1½ qt [1.4 L] store-bought chocolate chip ice cream (see Note)

If you're on the hunt for the best chocolate cookie, look no further. Filled with molten bursts of melted dark chocolate and studded with sweet white chocolate chips, these cookies are baked to perfection with crisp, chewy edges and rich, fudgy centers—they're everything a chocolate cookie should be. In fact, they feel so unbelievably decadent that I wrote the recipe as a small batch. Not to worry—it can easily be doubled when your chocolate craving knows no bounds.

TO MAKE THE COOKIES

Preheat the oven to 350°F [180°C]. Line two baking sheets with parchment paper or silicone baking mats.

In a medium bowl, stir together the flour, cocoa powder, baking soda, baking powder, and salt. Set aside.

In the bowl of a stand mixer fitted with the paddle attachment, mix together the butter, brown sugar, and granulated sugar on medium-high speed for 2 to 3 minutes, or until light and fluffy. Add the egg and vanilla, mixing to combine well. Add the flour mixture and mix on low speed until combined.

Remove the bowl from the stand mixer and stir in the chocolate chunks and white chocolate chips with a large spatula or wooden spoon. Let the dough sit for 10 minutes at room temperature to firm up a bit.

cont.

NOTE

If using store-bought ice cream, prepare it ahead of time: Soften the ice cream at room temperature and use a large spatula to spread it into a parchment lined 9 by 13 in [23 by 33 cm] baking pan. Use an offset spatula to level the top, working quickly so that the ice cream doesn't melt completely. Freeze overnight.

Use a 2 tablespoon cookie scoop to transfer the dough to the prepared baking sheets, leaving 2 to 3 in [5 to 7.5 cm] between each cookie. Bake for 10 to 12 minutes, or until the edges are set and the cookies are slightly puffed up in the center. Do not overbake or the cookies will be dry. Halfway through the baking cycle, remove each pan from the oven and tap it firmly twice on the countertop to flatten the cookies. Rotate the pans and continue baking.

Remove the pans from the oven and let the cookies cool on the baking sheets for 15 minutes before using a spatula to carefully transfer the cookies to a wire cooling rack to cool completely. If time allows, freeze the cookies for 30 minutes before making the ice cream sandwiches.

TO ASSEMBLE THE ICE CREAM SANDWICHES

Use a round cookie cutter the same size as the cookies to cut rounds of chocolate chip ice cream from the pan. Place an ice cream round on the flat side of a cookie and top with a second cookie, flat-side down. Gently press together to form a sandwich. Repeat with the remaining cookies and ice cream.

Immediately place the ice cream sandwiches in the freezer to set. Freeze for at least 2 hours or, for best results, overnight.

Store the cookies (without ice cream) in an airtight container for up to 4 days. Once the ice cream sandwiches are assembled, keep tightly wrapped in the freezer for up to 2 months.

ROOT BEER POPCORN COOKIE ICE CREAM SANDWICHES

ROOT BEER POPCORN

2 cups [480 ml] root beer

4 cups [30 g] air-popped popcorn

3 tablespoons unsalted butter

½ cup [100 g] light brown sugar, packed

⅛ teaspoon kosher salt

COOKIES

2¼ cups [280 g] all-purpose flour, spooned and leveled

½ teaspoon baking powder

½ teaspoon baking soda

½ teaspoon kosher salt

¾ cup [170 g] unsalted butter, at room temperature

1 cup [200 g] light brown sugar, packed

¼ cup [50 g] granulated sugar

1 egg, at room temperature

1 teaspoon vanilla extract

FOR ASSEMBLY

1 recipe Slow-Churn Vanilla Ice Cream (page 262), or 1½ qt [1.4 L] store-bought vanilla ice cream (see Note)

My inspiration for these popcorn-filled cookies comes from Joanne Chang's *Pastry Love*. If you don't think that popcorn belongs in a cookie, this recipe will prove you wrong. They're a bit more time-consuming than most cookie sandwiches, but they're also a lot of fun, and the end result is nothing short of totally addictive. My book club friends beg for this cookie, and it's worth the extra steps needed to create it.

TO MAKE THE ROOT BEER POPCORN
In a medium saucepan over medium-low heat, simmer the root beer until reduced to ½ cup [120 ml]. This will take about 25 minutes. Once reduced, remove from the heat and transfer the root beer to a small bowl to cool slightly.

Adjust the oven rack to the center position and preheat the oven to 325°F [165°C]. Line a baking sheet with parchment paper or a silicone baking mat.

Place the air-popped popcorn in a large bowl.

In a small saucepan over medium heat, melt the butter. Once melted, add the brown sugar and cook, stirring, until the mixture begins to bubble and thicken. Continue stirring for 1 to 2 minutes, or until the color deepens. Stir in the reduced root beer and bring it to near boiling. Continue stirring until the mixture thickens significantly, 10 to 12 minutes. Remove the pan from the heat and stir in the salt. Allow to cool for 2 to 3 minutes.

cont.

Pour the root beer mixture over the popcorn and use a large spoon or spatula to stir it together until all the popcorn is coated evenly.

Transfer the popcorn to the prepared baking sheet. Use the spoon or spatula to gently spread it evenly across the baking sheet.

Bake for 12 to 15 minutes, or until most of the liquid is absorbed into the popcorn, rotating the baking sheet halfway through. Remove the popcorn from the oven and let cool for at least 30 minutes before adding to the cookie dough. The popcorn will be soft at first but will become crunchy as it cools. Once cool, use your hands to break up any large pieces.

To store the popcorn to use later, place it in a large plastic storage bag for up to 5 days.

TO MAKE THE COOKIES
Preheat the oven to 350°F [180°C] and line two baking sheets with parchment paper or silicone baking mats.

In a medium bowl, whisk together the flour, baking powder, baking soda, and salt.

In the bowl of a stand mixer fitted with the paddle attachment, cream together the butter, brown sugar, and granulated sugar until light and fluffy, about 3 minutes. Add the egg followed by the vanilla, and mix until well combined. Add the flour mixture and mix on low speed until combined. Stop when there are only a few streaks of flour remaining.

Remove the bowl from the mixer and use a sturdy spatula or wooden spoon to scrape down the sides of the bowl. Stir in the root beer popcorn. Do not overmix.

Cover the bowl and chill the dough for 10 minutes.

Use a 2 tablespoon cookie scoop to scoop the dough onto the prepared baking sheets, leaving 2 in [5 cm] between each cookie.

Bake for 10 to 11 minutes, or until the edges of the cookies are just barely golden brown and the centers are set but not overbaked. Remove from the oven and allow the cookies to cool on the baking sheet for 10 minutes before using a spatula to carefully transfer the cookies to a wire cooling rack to cool completely.

TO ASSEMBLE THE ICE CREAM SANDWICHES
Use a cookie cutter the same size as the cookies to cut out rounds of vanilla ice cream from the pan. Place an ice cream round on the flat side of one cookie and top with a second cookie, flat-side down. Gently press together to form a sandwich. Repeat with the remaining cookies and ice cream. Place the sandwiches in the freezer for a minimum of 2 hours or overnight.

Store the cookies (without ice cream) in an airtight container for up to 4 days. Once the ice cream sandwiches are assembled, keep tightly wrapped in the freezer for up to 2 months.

TART & TANGY

LAVENDER LEMON SHORTBREAD
WITH
MEYER LEMON CURD

I've always loved the combination of lemon and lavender. You'll want to bookmark this recipe not just because the cookies are positively scrumptious, but because you'll want to spread the Meyer lemon curd on top of everything in your kitchen. Or do as I do and eat it by the spoonful straight from the jar.

LAVENDER LEMON SHORTBREAD

1¾ cups [220 g] all-purpose flour, spooned and leveled

½ teaspoon fine sea salt

⅓ cup [65 g] granulated sugar

Zest of 1 Meyer lemon

10 tablespoons [145 g] unsalted butter, at room temperature

1 egg yolk, at room temperature

1 teaspoon finely ground culinary lavender

FOR ASSEMBLY

Confectioners' sugar, for dusting

1 recipe Meyer Lemon Curd (page 258, see Note)

TO MAKE THE SHORTBREAD

In a medium bowl, whisk together the flour and salt. Set aside.

In the bowl of a stand mixer fitted with the paddle attachment, combine the sugar and lemon zest and use your fingers to mix until the zest is evenly spread throughout the sugar. Add the butter and beat on medium-low speed for 1 to 2 minutes, or until pale and creamy. Add the egg yolk and lavender. Mix until combined well. Add the flour mixture and mix on low speed until combined. The dough will be crumbly and sandy in texture.

Lay a 12 in [30.5 cm] strip of plastic wrap on your work surface. Transfer the dough to the middle of the plastic wrap. Wrap the dough in the plastic wrap, using the plastic wrap to help press dough together into a flat disk shape about 1½ in [4 cm] thick. Place the tightly wrapped disk of dough in the refrigerator for at least 2 hours (or overnight).

Line two baking sheets with parchment paper or silicone baking mats. Place in the refrigerator to chill. (It is important to keep the baking sheet and dough on the colder side to help hold the cookie cutter shape.)

cont.

NOTES

The Meyer Lemon Curd has to
be made in advance, so plan
ahead.

Once the dough is chilled, lightly flour your work surface and the rolling pin. Roll out the dough to ¼ in [6 mm] thick. If you do not have a linzer cookie cutter, use a 2 in [5 cm] round cookie cutter to make the cookie shape. To create the window in the top of the linzer cookie, use a piping tip, or anything that is ¾ in [2 cm] in diameter, to cut out the center of half of the cookies so they look like donuts. Place the cookies, 1 to 2 in [2.5 to 5 cm] apart, on a chilled baking sheet and place in the refrigerator for about 10 minutes.

After you have rolled out the dough for the first time and cut out as many cookies as possible, gather the scraps (including the cutout "donut" middles) and form another flat disk shape. Wrap the disk in plastic wrap and place in the refrigerator again for 15 minutes to firm up. Repeat this process until all the cookie dough has been used. Make sure you have an even number of round cookies (the bottoms) and "donut" cookies (the tops); you should have 18 of each.

While the cookies are chilling in the refrigerator, adjust the oven rack to the middle position and preheat the oven to 350°F [180°C].

When the oven is ready, use a fork to prick the top of each solid cookie a few times (only the bottoms, not the "donut" tops). Bake for 10 to 13 minutes. Remove from the oven when the edges are just starting to turn golden. Let cool on the baking sheet for 5 minutes before using a spatula to carefully transfer the cookies to a wire cooling rack. Let cool completely before adding the lemon curd.

TO ASSEMBLE THE COOKIE SANDWICHES

Line up all the cookie "donut" tops, flat-side down. Dust with confectioners' sugar. Use a piping bag, or a teaspoon, to add about 1½ teaspoons of the Meyer Lemon Curd to each of the cookie bottoms. Carefully place a sugar-covered cookie on top of each one and press gently to seal the lemon curd inside.

The shortbread will keep for 1 week in an airtight container at room temperature. The cookie sandwiches are best eaten on the day they are assembled. I recommend making the cookies and the curd a day or two ahead of time and assembling the sandwiches just before eating.

LEMON POPPY SEED COOKIES
WITH
MEYER LEMON CURD AND VANILLA BUTTERCREAM

LEMON POPPY SEED COOKIES

2½ cups [315 g] all-purpose flour, spooned and leveled

1 tablespoon poppy seeds

1 teaspoon baking soda

1 teaspoon cream of tartar

½ teaspoon salt

¾ cup [170 g] unsalted butter, room temperature

1 cup [200 g] granulated sugar

½ cup [100 g] light brown sugar, packed

1 tablespoon lemon zest

1 egg, plus one egg yolk

1½ teaspoons vanilla extract

FOR ASSEMBLY

1 recipe Vanilla Buttercream (page 246)

1 recipe Meyer Lemon Curd (page 258, see Note), cold

There simply aren't enough words in the English dictionary to describe just how much I love these lemon poppy seed cookies. The cookies themselves are bursting with fresh citrus flavor, and the bright lemon curd center is like a bite of edible sunshine. I insist you move these to the tippy-top of your must-bake list. Don't chase perfection when assembling these cookie sandwiches. Just lick your fingers and move along with your day.

TO MAKE THE COOKIES
In a medium bowl, combine the flour, poppy seeds, baking soda, cream of tartar, and salt. Whisk together and set aside.

In the bowl of a stand mixer fitted with the paddle attachment, combine the butter, granulated sugar, brown sugar, and lemon zest. Mix on medium speed for about 3 minutes, or until light and fluffy. Add the egg and egg yolk, one at a time, stopping the mixer and scraping down the sides of the bowl between additions. Add the vanilla and mix until well combined. Add the flour mixture in two additions, mixing on low speed after each addition, until just combined. Do not overmix.

Cover the dough and chill in the refrigerator for 2 hours or overnight.

cont.

NOTES

The Meyer Lemon Curd has to
be made in advance, so plan
ahead.

Once chilled, preheat the oven to 350°F [180°C]. Line two baking sheets with parchment paper or silicone baking mats. Using a 2 tablespoon cookie scoop, portion out the dough onto the prepared baking sheets, 2 in [5 cm] apart.

Bake for 9 to 11 minutes, or until the edges are golden brown and the centers of the cookies are just barely set.

Remove from the oven and let the cookies cool on the baking sheets for 5 minutes before using a spatula to carefully transfer the cookies to a wire cooling rack. Let cool completely before assembling the cookie sandwiches.

TO ASSEMBLE THE COOKIE SANDWICHES

Transfer the Vanilla Buttercream to a piping bag. Pipe a swirl of buttercream around the outside edge of the flat side of a cookie, leaving the center open. Place 2 teaspoons of the Meyer Lemon Curd in the center of the buttercream circle. Top with a second cookie, flat-side down, and gently press together to form a sandwich. Repeat with the remaining cookies and filling. Place the cookie sandwiches in the refrigerator for 20 minutes to set.

The cookies will keep for 1 week in an airtight container at room temperature. Once assembled, the cookie sandwiches are best eaten the day they are made. I recommend making the cookies, buttercream, and curd a day or two ahead of time, and then assembling the sandwiches just before eating.

KEY LIME PIE SANDWICH COOKIES

KEY LIME COOKIES

1¾ cups [220 g] all-purpose flour, spooned and leveled

1½ cups [175 g] fine graham cracker crumbs

1 teaspoon baking soda

¾ teaspoon kosher salt

¾ cup [170 g] unsalted butter, at room temperature

1 cup [200 g] light brown sugar, packed

¼ cup [50 g] granulated sugar

2 eggs, at room temperature

1 teaspoon vanilla extract

FOR ASSEMBLY

1 recipe Key Lime Pie Cream Cheese Filling (page 259)

Zest of 1 lime (optional)

My husband lives for these cookies. They are an ode to the classic key lime pie, which is his favorite dessert. The tart key lime filling is a perfect match for the buttery graham cracker cookies. If you can't find key limes, go ahead and use regular limes. No one will know the difference.

TO MAKE THE COOKIES
In a medium bowl, combine the flour, graham cracker crumbs, baking soda, and salt. Whisk together and set aside.

In the bowl of a stand mixer fitted with the paddle attachment, cream together the butter, brown sugar, and granulated sugar until light and fluffy, 3 to 4 minutes. Stop the mixer and scrape down the sides of the bowl. Add the eggs, one at a time, mixing until incorporated. Add the vanilla and mix to combine well.

With the mixer on low speed, add the dry ingredients to the butter mixture in two additions. Mix until just combined. Cover the bowl with plastic wrap and refrigerate for 3 hours or overnight.

Once the dough is chilled, preheat the oven to 350°F [180°C]. Line two baking sheets with parchment paper or silicone baking mats. Using a 2 tablespoon cookie scoop, scoop uniform rounds of dough onto the prepared baking sheets, 2 in [5 cm] apart.

Bake for 8 to 9 minutes, or until the cookie edges are golden brown. Remove from the oven and let the cookies cool on the baking sheet for 5 minutes before using a spatula to carefully transfer the cookies to a wire cooling rack to cool completely.

cont.

TO ASSEMBLE THE COOKIE SANDWICHES

Transfer the Key Lime Pie Cream Cheese Filling to a piping bag fitted with a star tip. Turn half of the cookies over and pipe 2 tablespoons of filling onto the flat side of the cookies. Sprinkle with zest, if desired. Top each cookie with a second cookie, flat-side down, gently pressing together to form sandwiches.

Store tightly covered in the refrigerator for up to 4 days.

ALMOND LINZER COOKIES
WITH
TART CHERRY JAM

2½ cups [315 g] all-purpose flour, spooned and leveled, plus more as needed

1¼ cups [150 g] finely ground almond flour, spooned and leveled

⅓ cup [45 g] cornstarch

½ teaspoon salt

1 cup [226 g] unsalted butter, at room temperature

¾ cup [150 g] granulated sugar

2 eggs, at room temperature

1 teaspoon vanilla extract

1 teaspoon almond extract

¼ cup [30 g] confectioners' sugar, for dusting

FOR ASSEMBLY

½ cup [150 g] cherry jam

These sugar-dusted shortbread cookies could not be easier to make, yet they ooze fanciness. The hint of almond in the dough pairs nicely with any number of fillings, from strawberry jam to lemon curd. The cookies will soften as they sit with the filling, so if you prefer a crisper cookie, assemble them just before serving.

TO MAKE THE COOKIES
In a medium bowl, sift together the all-purpose flour, almond flour, cornstarch, and salt. Whisk to combine. Set aside.

In the bowl of a stand mixer fitted with the paddle attachment, mix together the butter and sugar until light and fluffy. Stop the mixer and scrape down the sides of the bowl with a spatula. Add the eggs, one at a time, and mix until fully incorporated. Add the vanilla and almond extract and mix to combine. Gradually add the flour mixture, mixing on low speed for 2 to 3 minutes, or until the dough begins to pull away from the sides of the bowl and gather in a ball. If the dough is too wet, add 1 to 2 tablespoons all-purpose flour.

Transfer the dough to your work surface and divide it in half. Wrap one half in plastic wrap and set aside. Use a rolling pin to roll the other half of the dough between two large pieces of parchment paper until no more than ¼ in [6 mm] thick. (To keep the parchment from sliding on the countertop, place it on top of a silicone baking mat.) Repeat with the second half of the dough. Stack the parchment-covered dough slabs one on top of the other on a baking sheet and refrigerate for 30 minutes, or until firm.

cont.

Meanwhile, adjust the oven rack to the middle position and preheat the oven to 350°F [180°C]. Line two baking sheets with parchment paper or silicone baking mats.

Remove the rolled-out dough from the refrigerator and use a 2 in [5 cm] linzer or round cookie cutter to cut the dough into rounds. Use the small center piece or a ½ in [13 mm] round cookie cutter to cut a hole in the center of half of the cookies.

Use a metal spatula to transfer the shapes to the prepared baking sheets. Arrange the cookies about 1 in [2.5 cm] apart. The dough will not spread while baking. If baking one baking sheet at a time, place the other cut-out cookies in the refrigerator until ready to bake. Gather up the scraps of dough and continue rolling and cutting rounds until all the dough has been used and you have 48 cookies (24 solid bottoms and 24 windowed tops).

Bake for 8 to 9 minutes, or until the edges are set. The cookies will be slightly golden brown on the bottom but not on the edges or tops of the cookies.

Remove the cookies from the oven and allow to cool on the pan for 5 minutes before using a spatula to carefully transfer them to a wire cooling rack. Let cool completely before assembling the cookie sandwiches.

TO ASSEMBLE THE COOKIE SANDWICHES
Line up the windowed top cookies and dust them with confectioners' sugar. Spread 1 teaspoon of cherry jam on each of the solid cookies. Carefully place the sugar-dusted tops over the jam to form sandwiches.

The cookies will keep for 1 week in an airtight container at room temperature. The cookie sandwiches are best eaten the day they are assembled.

HOMEMADE VIENNESE WHIRLS
WITH
STRAWBERRY JAM AND VANILLA BUTTERCREAM

VIENNESE WHIRLS

1¾ cups [220 g] all-purpose flour, spooned and leveled

1 tablespoon cornstarch

1 cup [226 g] unsalted butter, at room temperature (see Notes)

½ cup [50 g] sifted confectioners' sugar, plus more for dusting

2 teaspoons vanilla extract

FOR ASSEMBLY

1 recipe Vanilla Buttercream (page 246)

1 recipe Homemade Strawberry Jam (page 261, see Notes)

There is a bakery in our local town that makes the most delightful Viennese whirls. Every year my husband picks up a tray on the way home from work just before the holidays. I always say it simply isn't Christmas without them. Just like the British classic, these are filled with a fluffy vanilla buttercream and sweet homemade strawberry jam. They are as pretty as can be, garnished with a simple dusting of confectioners' sugar.

TO MAKE THE WHIRLS
Line two baking sheets with parchment paper or silicone baking mats. Use a 2 in [5 cm] cookie cutter to trace circles on the parchment paper. Space the circles out by 1½ to 2 in [4 to 5 cm].

In a medium bowl, whisk together the flour and cornstarch. Set aside.

In the bowl of a stand mixer fitted with the paddle attachment, beat the butter and confectioners' sugar on medium speed for about 2 minutes. Stop the mixer and scrape down the sides of the bowl, as needed. Mix in the vanilla. Add the flour mixture and mix on low speed for 30 to 60 seconds, or until the dough comes together.

cont.

Make the Homemade
Strawberry Jam ahead of
time, as it requires at least
3 hours to chill. If you're short
on time, substitute store-
bought strawberry jam.

For the cookies, the butter
should be very soft. For best
results, leave the butter out
overnight. This will help make
the dough easier to pipe.

Transfer the dough into a piping bag fitted with a large star tip. Pipe the dough onto the prepared parchment paper: On the inside of each circle, pipe the dough around in a spiral starting along the edge and ending in the middle of the circle, lifting the piping tip straight up.

Place the baking sheet in the refrigerator for 15 to 20 minutes. This helps the cookies keep their shape as they bake.

While the dough is chilling, adjust the oven rack to the middle position and preheat the oven to 375°F [190°C].

Remove the baking sheet from the refrigerator and bake the cookies for 13 to 15 minutes, or until the cookie edges are golden brown. Remove from the oven and let the cookies cool for 5 minutes on the baking sheet before using a spatula to carefully transfer the cookies to a wire cooling rack. Let cool completely before adding the filling.

TO ASSEMBLE THE COOKIE SANDWICHES

Transfer the Vanilla Buttercream to a piping bag fitted with a large tip. Line up half of the cookies and flip them over so that the flat side is facing up. Pipe the buttercream onto the flat side of one cookie and then dollop 1 tablespoon of the Homemade Strawberry Jam on top. Gently top with a second cookie, flat-side down, and gently press together to create a sandwich. Repeat with the remaining cookies, frosting, and jam. Dust the tops with confectioners' sugar, if desired.

You will have extra jam after filling the cookies. Store it tightly covered in the refrigerator and use on your morning toast or for a second batch of cookies.

The cookies will keep for 5 days in an airtight container at room temperature. Once the cookie sandwiches are assembled with jam and buttercream, they should be stored in the refrigerator and eaten within 2 days.

VANILLA BEAN SHORTBREAD
WITH
GUAVA BUTTERCREAM

VANILLA BEAN SHORTBREAD

3¾ cups [470 g] all-purpose flour, spooned and leveled

½ cup [70 g] cornstarch

½ teaspoon salt

1 cup [226 g] unsalted butter, at room temperature

¾ cup [150 g] granulated sugar

2 eggs, at room temperature

1 tablespoon vanilla bean paste

FOR ASSEMBLY

1 recipe Guava Buttercream (page 252, see Note)

There is nothing not to love about these sweet shortbread cookies filled with swirls of pretty pink buttercream. I like to use guava jam here for its unique flavor and color, but really, you can make a buttercream using whatever jam you have stashed in your pantry. This will be your signature springtime cookie.

TO MAKE THE SHORTBREAD

In a medium bowl, whisk together the flour, cornstarch, and salt.

In the bowl of a stand mixer fitted with the paddle attachment, mix together the butter and sugar until combined well. Stop the mixer and scrape down the sides of the bowl with a spatula. Add the eggs, one at a time, and mix until fully incorporated, scraping down the sides of the bowl after each addition. Add the vanilla bean paste and mix on low speed to combine. Add the flour mixture and mix on medium speed for 3 to 4 minutes, or until the dough comes together in a ball.

Transfer the dough to your work surface and divide it in half. Cover one half with plastic wrap and set aside. Roll out the other half between two pieces of parchment paper until ¼ in [6 mm] thick. Place the parchment-covered dough onto a baking sheet and refrigerate for about 30 minutes, until firm.

cont.

While the cookie dough chills, preheat the oven to 350°F [180°C]. Line two baking sheets with parchment paper or silicone baking mats.

Once the dough has chilled, use a 2 in [5 cm] round cookie cutter to cut the dough into rounds. Transfer the cutouts to one of the prepared baking sheets, leaving 1 in [2.5 cm] between each cookie.

Freeze the baking sheet of cookie dough for 10 minutes and then bake for 10 to 11 minutes until baked through. The short-bread will remain pale in color and will not brown on top or at the edges. Be careful not to overbake.

Remove the cookies from the oven and let cool on the baking sheet for 5 minutes before using a spatula to carefully transfer the cookies to a wire cooling rack. Let cool completely before adding the frosting.

Repeat with the remaining dough until all the dough has been used.

TO ASSEMBLE THE COOKIE SANDWICHES
Transfer the Guava Buttercream to a piping bag fitted with a large star tip. Pipe a swirl of buttercream onto the flat side of one cookie and then top with a second cookie, flat-side down. Gently press together to form a sandwich. Repeat with the remaining cookies and buttercream until all the sandwiches are made.

Store the cookie sandwiches tightly covered at room temperature for up to 4 days.

CHERRY, PISTACHIO, AND WHITE CHOCOLATE SHORTBREAD

WITH

VANILLA BEAN BUTTERCREAM

CHERRY, PISTACHIO, AND WHITE CHOCOLATE SHORTBREAD

1 cup [226 g] unsalted butter, at room temperature

¾ cup [90 g] confectioners' sugar, sifted

1 teaspoon vanilla extract

2¾ cups [345 g] all-purpose flour, spooned and leveled, plus more if needed

¼ teaspoon salt

½ cup [70 g] dried cherries, finely chopped

¾ cup [90 g] finely chopped pistachios

⅔ cup [95 g] chopped white chocolate

FOR ASSEMBLY

1 recipe Vanilla Buttercream (page 246)

½ cup [150 g] cherry jam

Filled with tart cherries, nutty pistachios, and creamy white chocolate, these cookies epitomize all that a holiday cookie should be. This classic shortbread will quickly become a seasonal favorite, especially if you love to entertain or host house guests. The dough can easily be frozen and baked off at a moment's notice.

TO MAKE THE SHORTBREAD

In the bowl of a stand mixer fitted with the paddle attachment, cream together the butter and confectioners' sugar on medium-high speed until light and fluffy, about 3 minutes. Add the vanilla and mix to combine. Add the flour and salt. Mix on low speed until the dough begins to pull away from the sides of the bowl and come together. If the dough feels very sticky, add 1 or 2 tablespoons flour.

Remove the bowl from the mixer and use a sturdy spatula or wooden spoon to stir in the cherries, ½ cup [60 g] of the pistachios, and the white chocolate chunks. Do not overmix.

cont.

Transfer the dough to your work surface and divide it in half. Wrap one half in plastic wrap and set aside. Use a rolling pin to roll the other half of the dough between two large pieces of parchment paper until it is ¼ to ½ in [6 to 13 mm] thick. (To keep the parchment paper from sliding on the countertop, place it on top of a silicone baking mat.) Repeat with the second half of the dough. Stack the parchment-lined dough slabs one on top of the other on a baking sheet and refrigerate for at least 2 hours.

When ready to bake the cookies, remove the dough from the refrigerator and preheat the oven to 350°F [180°C]. Line two baking sheets with parchment paper or silicone baking mats.

Place the remaining ¼ cup [30 g] of chopped pistachios in a shallow bowl. Use a 2 in [5 cm] round cookie cutter to cut rounds from the chilled dough. Carefully roll the edges of each cookie in the chopped pistachios and place 1 in [2.5 cm] apart on the prepared baking sheets. The cookies will not spread while baking.

Gather the scraps of dough and roll it flat again between the two pieces of parchment paper while it is still cold. Continue cutting circles until all the dough has been used.

Bake the cookies for 10 to 12 minutes, or until the edges are set, or longer for a crispier cookie. Remove the cookies from the oven and let cool on the baking sheet for 5 to 10 minutes before using a spatula to carefully transfer the cookies to a wire cooling rack to cool completely before assembling the cookie sandwiches.

TO ASSEMBLE THE COOKIE SANDWICHES
Transfer the Vanilla Bean Buttercream to a piping bag and pipe about 1 tablespoon onto the flat side of a cookie, and then dollop 1 to 2 teaspoons of cherry jam on top. Top with a second cookie, flat-side down, and gently press together to form a sandwich. Repeat with the remaining cookies and buttercream.

Store the cookies without buttercream tightly covered at room temperature for up to 5 days. Once assembled, the cookie sandwiches are best stored at room temperature for up to 3 days. You can also freeze the dough unbaked or the cookies after baking for up to 2 months.

CRANBERRY ORANGE COCONUT COOKIES

WITH

WHITE CHOCOLATE BUTTERCREAM

(CHRISTMAS MORNING COOKIES)

CRANBERRY ORANGE COCONUT COOKIES

1 cup [125 g] all-purpose flour, spooned and leveled

½ cup [65 g] whole-wheat flour, spooned and leveled (see Note)

½ cup [60 g] graham cracker crumbs

½ teaspoon baking soda

½ teaspoon baking powder

½ teaspoon ground cinnamon

½ teaspoon salt

1 tablespoon orange zest

¾ cup [150 g] cup granulated sugar

½ cup [100 g] light brown sugar, packed

10 tablespoons [145 g] unsalted butter, at room temperature

2 eggs, at room temperature

1 teaspoon vanilla extract

1 cup [140 g] dried cranberries, chopped

⅔ cup [57 g] sweetened shredded coconut

⅔ cup [80 g] chopped pecans, lightly toasted

FOR ASSEMBLY

1 recipe White Chocolate Buttercream (page 250)

Every year at Christmastime, my girls beg me to make their favorite cranberry bars, complete with a buttery graham cracker crust and notes of brown sugar and citrus. I knew I wanted to play around with that recipe and come up with a cookie version for the book. My youngest is one of those people who loves things the way they've always been, so imagine my delight when she said she loved this new take on her beloved bars! The cookie texture is soft, chewy, and utterly delicious; the white chocolate buttercream is a thing of magic—swirl it between two cranberry orange coconut cookies et voila, you win Christmas!

TO MAKE THE COOKIES
In a medium bowl, combine the all-purpose flour, whole-wheat flour, graham cracker crumbs, baking soda, baking powder, cinnamon, and salt. Whisk together and set aside.

cont.

NOTE

Instead of using whole wheat
flour, you can also use an
additional ½ cup [65 g] all-
purpose flour.

Place the orange zest in the bowl of a stand mixer fitted with the paddle attachment. Add the granulated sugar and use your hands to massage the sugar and zest together for about 30 seconds. Add the brown sugar and butter. Beat on medium-high speed for 2 to 3 minutes, or until light and fluffy. Stop the mixer and scrape down the sides of the bowl. Add the eggs and vanilla and mix until well combined. Scrape down the sides of the bowl once more. Add the flour mixture and mix on low speed until only a few streaks of flour remain.

Remove the bowl from the mixer and use a large spatula or wooden spoon to stir in the cranberries, coconut, and pecans by hand. Do not overmix.

Cover the dough and refrigerate for at least 2 hours or overnight.

When ready to bake the cookies, preheat the oven to 350°F [180°C]. Line two baking sheets with parchment paper or silicone baking mats.

Use a 2 tablespoon cookie scoop to scoop the dough onto the prepared baking sheets, leaving about 2 in [5 cm] between each cookie.

Bake for 9 to 10 minutes, or until the edges of the cookies are golden brown and the centers are puffed up and ever so slightly underbaked.

Remove from the oven. Let the cookies cool on the baking sheets for 10 minutes before using a spatula to carefully transfer the cookies to a wire cooling rack to cool completely before adding the filling.

TO ASSEMBLE THE COOKIE SANDWICHES
Transfer the White Chocolate Buttercream to a piping bag and pipe 1 to 2 tablespoons of buttercream onto the flat side of a cookie. Top with a second cookie, flat-side down, and gently press together to form a sandwich. Repeat with the remaining cookies and buttercream.

Store the cookies without buttercream tightly covered at room temperature for up to 3 days. Once assembled, the cookie sandwiches are best stored in the refrigerator for up to 3 days.

ORANGE BUTTER COOKIES
WITH
CHOCOLATE GANACHE

ORANGE BUTTER COOKIES

14 tablespoons [200 g] unsalted butter, at room temperature

¾ cup [90 g] confectioners' sugar, sifted

2 tablespoons light brown sugar, packed

1½ teaspoons vanilla extract

Zest of 1 orange

2 cups [250 g] all-purpose flour, spooned and leveled

1 tablespoon cold water, as needed

½ teaspoon kosher salt

½ cup [70 g] chopped semisweet chocolate

¼ cup [50 g] turbinado sugar

FOR ASSEMBLY

1 recipe Chocolate Ganache (page 245, see Note)

These buttery shortbread cookies are delightfully crisp and dotted with bits of chopped chocolate and fresh orange zest. Dusting the edges with a sprinkle of turbinado sugar gives these cookies a bit of sparkle, making them perfect for holiday gift giving.

TO MAKE THE COOKIES
In the bowl of stand mixer fitted with the paddle attachment, mix together the butter, confectioners' sugar, and brown sugar on medium-high speed until light and creamy, 2 to 3 minutes. Add the vanilla and orange zest and mix to combine. Add the flour and salt, mixing on low speed until the dough comes together. It will be slightly tacky. If the dough is dry, add up to 1 tablespoon cold water to help bring the dough together. Remove the bowl from the mixer and use a large spatula or wooden spoon to stir in the chopped chocolate. Do not overmix.

Transfer the dough to your work surface and divide it in half. Wrap one half in plastic wrap and set aside. Use a rolling pin to roll the other half of the dough between two large pieces of parchment paper until it is ¼ to ½ in [6 to 13 mm] thick. (To keep the parchment paper from sliding on your work surface, place it on top of a silicone baking mat.) Repeat with the second half of the dough. Stack the parchment-lined dough slabs one on top of the other on a baking sheet and refrigerate for 2 hours.

Remove the dough from the refrigerator and preheat the oven to 350°F [180°C]. Line two baking sheets with parchment paper or silicone baking mats. Place the turbinado sugar in a shallow bowl.

cont.

Use a 2 in [5 cm] round cookie or biscuit cutter to cut 28 to 32 rounds from the chilled dough. Carefully roll the outside edges of each cookie in the turbinado sugar. Place the cookies on the baking sheet 1 in [2.5 cm] apart. They will not spread while baking. Gather the scraps, reroll, and cut the dough until all the dough has been used.

Bake for 10 to 12 minutes until the edges are slightly golden brown, or longer for a crispier cookie.

Remove from the oven and let the cookies cool on the baking sheet for 10 minutes before using a spatula to carefully transfer them to a wire cooling rack to cool completely before adding the filling.

TO ASSEMBLE THE COOKIE SANDWICHES
Transfer the Chocolate Ganache to a piping bag. Pipe about 2 teaspoons onto the flat side of one cookie (or use an offset spatula to spread the ganache, if preferred). Top with a second cookie, flat-side down, and gently press together to form a sandwich. Repeat with remaining cookies and ganache. Chill for 20 to 30 minutes, or until the ganache has set.

Store the cookie sandwiches tightly covered in the refrigerator for up to 4 days.

STRAWBERRY SHORTCAKE MACARONS

VANILLA BEAN MACARONS

105 g finely ground almond flour

105 g confectioners' sugar

1 Tbsp [5 g] freeze-dried strawberry powder

½ vanilla bean

100 g egg whites (from about 3 eggs)

Pinch of cream of tartar (optional; for stabilizing the egg whites)

90 g superfine granulated sugar

Pink gel food coloring (optional)

FOR ASSEMBLY

1 recipe Vanilla Buttercream (page 246)

1 recipe Homemade Strawberry Jam (page 261, see Note), or ½ cup [200 g] store-bought strawberry jam

As pretty as they are delicious, these strawberry shortcake macarons will disappear quickly. If you run out of steam to make the strawberry jam from scratch, store-bought jam is a-okay!

TO MAKE THE MACARONS
Line two baking sheets with silicone mats printed with macaron templates. Alternatively, line the baking sheets with parchment paper that has been traced with 1½ in [4 cm] circles spaced 2 in [5 cm] apart. Set aside.

In a large bowl, sift together the almond flour, confectioners' sugar, and freeze-dried strawberry powder through a fine-mesh sieve four times. Discard any pieces left in the sieve.

Scrape the inside of the vanilla bean to remove the seeds. Add the seeds to the flour mixture. Set aside.

In the bowl of a stand mixer fitted with the whisk attachment, mix the egg whites on medium-high speed until light and foamy, about 1 minute. Add the cream of tartar, if using, and slowly add the granulated sugar, 1 tablespoon at a time, while continuing to whisk on medium-high speed. Wait 10 to 15 seconds between each addition to be sure the sugar is incorporated. After all the sugar has been added, continue to beat the egg whites on medium-high speed until stiff peaks form. If adding gel food coloring, do so just before mixing is complete. The egg whites should be thick and fluffy and hold their shape when the whisk is turned upright. Be careful not to overmix.

cont.

NOTE

Make the Homemade
Strawberry Jam ahead of
time, as it requires at least
3 hours to chill. If short on
time, substitute store-bought
strawberry jam.

Once the egg whites hold stiff peaks, add half of the almond flour mixture to the egg whites and use a spatula to fold together. Do not stir the mixture but rather fold the ingredients together using broad, sweeping motions from the bottom of the bowl to the top. Before incorporating fully, add the other half of the dry ingredients and continue the folding motion. Pause to press the batter firmly against the sides of the bowl every now and then to smooth the batter.

Continue folding until the batter begins to flow like lava and you can lift the spatula in a figure-8 motion without the mixture breaking off. If it falls off, continue mixing for three or four folds at a time, then test again. Do not overmix, as your batter will become runny and the macarons will not bake properly.

Scoop the batter into a piping bag or thick plastic bag fitted with a ½ in [13 mm] plain tip. Pipe the macaron batter onto the prepared templates. Circles should measure 1¼ to 1½ in [3 to 4 cm]. When piping, hold the tip perpendicular to the baking sheet and apply pressure to the top of the piping bag to keep a continuous flow of batter. Release the pressure and use a small flick of the hand to end the flow of batter and leave a smooth top on the macaron.

Repeat with the remaining batter. Tap each baking sheet firmly on the countertop three times to release any air bubbles.

Allow the macarons to rest at room temperature for 30 to 60 minutes, or until the tops of the cookies are dry to the touch. Depending on the weather, this can take over an hour. Do not skip this step.

Meanwhile, adjust the oven rack to the lower center position and preheat the oven to 325°F [165°C].

Once dry, place a single sheet of macarons in the preheated oven and bake for 13 minutes, rotating halfway through. The macarons are done when the tops are firm and remain attached to the "feet," or base, when touched. Repeat with the remaining macarons.

Let cool on the baking sheet for 6 to 8 minutes before carefully transferring the macarons to a wire rack to cool completely. Repeat with the remaining macarons.

TO ASSEMBLE THE MACARONS

Transfer the Vanilla Buttercream to a piping bag and pipe
a small swirl of the buttercream onto the flat side of a
macaron, leaving the center open. Use a teaspoon to place
a dollop of the Homemade Strawberry Jam in the center of
the frosting. Top with a second macaron, flat-side down.
Very gently press the two together to seal. Repeat with
the remaining cookies, and then place all the macarons
in the refrigerator to set. The macarons are best stored in
the refrigerator and taste best the day after they are made.

COOKIES WITH A KICK

BROWN BUTTER SNICKERDOODLES
WITH
CHAI SPICE BUTTERCREAM

BROWN BUTTER SNICKERDOODLES

2¼ cups [280 g] all-purpose flour, spooned and leveled

1¼ teaspoons cream of tartar

1 teaspoon baking soda

1½ teaspoons ground cinnamon

¼ teaspoon fine sea salt

1 cup [226 g] unsalted butter

1¼ cups [250 g] granulated sugar, plus more for sprinkling

⅓ cup [65 g] light brown sugar, packed

2 eggs, at room temperature

1 teaspoon vanilla extract

FOR ASSEMBLY

1 recipe Chai Spice Buttercream (page 254)

Is it just me, or does saying the word *snickerdoodle* just make you smile every time? Let's try it together. Snicker-doodle. *Snick-errrr-doooodle.* Yep. Instant grins. The addition of brown butter and chai spice makes this one cozy cookie that pairs perfectly with fuzzy slippers and a warm blanket by the fire.

TO MAKE THE SNICKERDOODLES
In a medium bowl, whisk together the flour, cream of tartar, baking soda, 1 teaspoon of the cinnamon, and the salt. Set aside.

In a medium saucepan over medium-high heat, melt the butter, stirring occasionally. When the butter begins to crackle and pop, stir continuously. After about 5 minutes, the butter will form a layer of foam over the top and the crackling will stop. Continue to stir the butter as it browns. Amber-brown butter solids will collect on the bottom of the pan and the butter will smell slightly nutty and be amber in color. Remove from the heat, pour into the bowl of a stand mixer fitted with the paddle attachment, and allow to cool for 10 minutes.

cont.

Once the butter is cool, add 1 cup [200 g] of the granulated sugar and the brown sugar to the bowl. Mix on medium-low speed about 2 minutes, until light and fluffy. Stop the mixer and scrape down the sides of the bowl. Add the eggs and mix until combined. Mix in the vanilla. Add the dry ingredients to the stand mixer and mix on low speed for 30 to 60 seconds, or until the dough comes together.

Place the dough in the refrigerator for about 20 minutes. This helps firm up the dough just a bit, to make it easier to roll into balls.

While the cookie dough is chilling, adjust the oven rack to the middle position and preheat the oven to 350°F [180°C]. Line two baking sheets with parchment paper or silicone baking mats. Combine the remaining ¼ cup [50 g] of sugar and ½ teaspoon of cinnamon in a small bowl.

Remove the cookie dough from the refrigerator. Scoop the dough into 2½ tablespoon portions and roll each between your hands to form a uniform ball. Generously coat each ball in the cinnamon sugar. Place the rolled cookie dough balls on the prepared baking sheets and then gently use your finger to make an indentation in the middle of each cookie. Sprinkle with a little more sugar.

Bake for 9 to 11 minutes, or until the edges are set. Let the cookies cool on the baking sheets for 10 minutes before using a spatula to carefully transfer the cookies to a wire cooling rack. Let cool completely before adding the filling.

TO ASSEMBLE THE COOKIE SANDWICHES

Transfer the Chai Spice Buttercream to a piping bag. Line up half of the baked cookies and flip them over so they're flat-side up. Pipe about 2 tablespoons of buttercream onto the flat side of each cookie. Top with a second cookie, flat-side down, and gently press together to form a sandwich. Repeat with the remaining cookies and buttercream.

Store the cookie sandwiches tightly covered at room temperature for up to 3 days.

MAPLE SHORTBREAD
WITH
VANILLA BEAN BUTTERCREAM

MAPLE SHORTBREAD

1¾ cups [220 g] all-purpose flour, spooned and leveled

1 tablespoon cornstarch

½ teaspoon kosher salt

¾ cup [170 g] unsalted butter, at room temperature

½ cup [100 g] granulated sugar

¾ teaspoon maple extract

½ cup [150 g] turbinado sugar

FOR ASSEMBLY

1 recipe Vanilla Buttercream (page 246)

These slice 'n' bake shortbread cookies are just as perfect for a holiday cookie box as they are for a random Tuesday night on the sofa. Covered in a halo of turbinado sugar and filled with a sweet vanilla bean buttercream, these delightfully crispy cookie sandwiches literally melt in your mouth. I love these freshly made, but they're equally delicious days later.

TO MAKE THE SHORTBREAD
In a medium bowl, whisk together the flour, cornstarch, and salt.

In the bowl of a stand mixer fitted with the paddle attachment, mix the butter, granulated sugar, and maple extract on medium speed until light and fluffy, about 3 minutes. Stop the mixer and scrape down the sides of the bowl. Add the flour mixture in two additions, mixing on low speed after each addition until just combined. Do not overmix.

Transfer the dough onto a lightly floured surface and use your hands to form the dough into two equal halves. Mold each half into a log, 1½ to 2 in [4 to 5 cm] thick. Wrap each log in plastic wrap and refrigerate for 3 hours or overnight.

Once the dough is chilled, preheat the oven to 350°F [180°C]. Line two baking sheets with parchment paper or silicone baking mats. Place the turbinado sugar in a small bowl.

cont.

Take the dough logs out of the refrigerator and remove the plastic wrap. Use a sharp knife to cut ¼ in [6 mm] thick slices, turning the log as you go so as not to flatten out one side. Roll the edges of each slice in the turbinado sugar, covering thoroughly. Place the cookies on the prepared baking sheets, 1 in [2.5 cm] apart. Freeze the cookies on the pans for 10 minutes.

Remove the baking sheets from the freezer and bake for 16 to 18 minutes, until the edges of the shortbread are a light and golden brown and the centers are completely set. Remove the cookies from the oven and let them cool on the baking sheet for 5 to 10 minutes before using a spatula to carefully transfer them to a wire cooling rack. Let cool completely before assembling the sandwiches.

TO ASSEMBLE THE COOKIE SANDWICHES
Transfer the Vanilla Bean Buttercream to a piping bag. Turn half the cookies over. Pipe 2 teaspoons of buttercream in the center of the flat sides. Top each with a second cookie, flat-side down, and press together gently.

Store tightly covered in a cool, dry place for up to 5 days. These cookie sandwiches freeze beautifully tightly wrapped in two layers of plastic wrap. Defrost at room temperature before serving.

SNOWFLAKE CUT-OUT COOKIES
WITH
EGGNOG BUTTERCREAM

1½ cups [190 g] all-purpose flour, spooned and leveled

1 teaspoon baking powder

¼ teaspoon fine sea salt

½ cup [113 g] unsalted butter, at room temperature

½ cup [100 g] granulated sugar

1 egg, at room temperature

1½ teaspoons vanilla extract

FOR ASSEMBLY

1 recipe Eggnog Buttercream (page 253)

Snowflake cut-outs remind me so much of my childhood. Growing up, my mom would bake the cookies and let my sister and me decorate the tops with icing and sprinkles. These cookies are a little time-consuming to make but always worth the effort. If you can roll out cookie dough and operate a mixer, you can easily turn out these show-stopping cookies like a baking champ. Serve alongside a hot toddy or spiced cider for an extra-festive treat.

TO MAKE THE COOKIES
In a medium bowl, whisk together the flour, baking powder, and salt.

In the bowl of a stand mixer fitted with the paddle attachment, beat the butter and sugar on medium-low speed for about 3 minutes. Stop the mixer and scrape down the sides of the bowl as needed. Add the egg and mix on medium-low speed until combined. Add the vanilla and mix to combine. Scrape down the sides of the bowl once more. Add the flour mixture and mix on low speed for 30 to 60 seconds, or until the dough comes together.

Transfer the dough to a lightly floured surface and divide it in half. Form two flat disks and transfer each to the middle of a sheet of plastic wrap. Tightly wrap the dough in the plastic and place both disks in the refrigerator for at least 1 hour or overnight.

Adjust the oven rack to the middle position and preheat the oven to 400°F [200°C]. Line a baking sheet with parchment paper or a silicone baking mat.

cont.

Once the dough is chilled, lightly flour your work surface. Add a small amount of flour to the rolling pin to prevent the dough from sticking. Roll out one of the disks of dough to ¼ in [6 mm] thick. Use a 2½ in [6 cm] snowflake cookie cutter to cut out cookies and transfer to the prepared baking sheet. Place in the freezer for 10 to 15 minutes.

Remove the snowflake cookies from the freezer and bake for 6 to 7 minutes; the bottom edges of the cookies will turn slightly golden brown. Remove from the oven and let the cookies cool on the baking sheet for 10 minutes before using a spatula to carefully transfer the cookies to a wire cooling rack to cool completely before adding the filling.

Gather the scraps and continue to roll, cut out, chill, and bake until you've used up all the dough and you have 36 to 40 cookies.

TO ASSEMBLE THE COOKIE SANDWICHES

Transfer the Eggnog Buttercream to a piping bag. Flip half of the cooled cookies over so that they're flat-side up. Pipe 2 teaspoons of buttercream onto the flat side of a cookie. Top with a second cookie, flat-side down, and gently press together to form a sandwich. Repeat with the remaining cookies and buttercream. If desired, decorate the tops of the cookie sandwiches with royal icing or Vanilla Buttercream and top with sprinkles or sanding sugar.

Store the cookie sandwiches tightly covered at room temperature for up to 4 days.

SPICED CHOCOLATE COOKIES
WITH
DULCE DE LECHE

1⅓ cups [165 g] all-purpose flour, spooned and leveled

½ cup [40 g] Dutch-process cocoa powder, sifted

¾ teaspoon ground cinnamon

½ teaspoon espresso powder

½ teaspoon baking soda

½ teaspoon kosher salt

⅛ teaspoon cayenne pepper

½ cup [113 g] unsalted butter, at room temperature

1½ cups plus 2 tablespoons [330 g] granulated sugar

2 eggs, at room temperature

1 teaspoon vanilla extract

FOR ASSEMBLY

1 recipe Dulce de Leche (page 242), chilled (see Note)

Flaky salt, for sprinkling (optional)

If you've never had a spiced chocolate cookie, you're in for a pleasant surprise! These dark chocolate cookies are boldly flavored with a trifecta of cinnamon, cayenne, and espresso. They're affectionately known in our house as "cookies with a kick" (the inspiration for this chapter's name!). Made extra indulgent with a layer of dulce de leche, they're also delicious paired with cold vanilla ice cream.

TO MAKE THE COOKIES
Adjust the oven rack to the middle position and preheat the oven to 350°F [180°C]. Line two baking sheets with parchment paper or silicone baking mats.

In a medium bowl, whisk together the flour, cocoa powder, cinnamon, espresso powder, baking soda, salt, and cayenne.

In the bowl of a stand mixer fitted with the paddle attachment, cream together the butter and 1½ cups [300 g] of the sugar on medium speed until light and pale in color, about 3 minutes. Stop the mixer and scrape down the sides of the bowl. Add the eggs, one at a time, mixing for about 20 seconds after each addition. Mix in the vanilla. Add the flour mixture in two additions, mixing on low speed after each until incorporated. Do not overmix.

cont.

Remove the bowl from the stand mixer and use a sturdy spatula to give the dough a few more turns, scraping the bottom of the bowl to be sure all the ingredients are thoroughly mixed. Refrigerate for 15 minutes to let the dough firm up a bit.

Use a 3 tablespoon cookie scoop to portion out mounds of dough 2 to 3 in [5 to 7.5 cm] apart onto the prepared baking sheets. They will spread while baking. Sprinkle the tops with the remaining 2 tablespoons of sugar.

Bake for 11 to 12 minutes, or until the edges are set and the cookies are crackled on top. They may look slightly puffed up but will deflate as they cool, creating a flat cookie.

Remove the cookies from the oven and allow to cool on the baking sheet for 10 minutes before using a spatula to carefully transfer the cookies to a wire cooling rack to cool completely before assembling the cookie sandwiches.

TO ASSEMBLE THE COOKIE SANDWICHES
Place 2 to 3 teaspoons of chilled Dulce de Leche on the flat side of a cookie. Top with a second cookie, flat-side down, and gently press together. Repeat with the remaining cookies and Dulce de Leche. Refrigerate the sandwiches if the Dulce de Leche is soft.

Store the cookie sandwiches tightly covered in the refrigerator for up to 4 days. Bring to room temperature and sprinkle with flaky salt, if desired, before serving.

GINGERDOODLE NEAPOLITAN COOKIES
WITH
CINNAMON BUTTERCREAM

CINNAMON SUGAR TOPPING

¼ cup [50 g] granulated sugar

½ teaspoon ground cinnamon

Pinch of salt

GINGER COOKIES

2½ cups [315 g] all-purpose flour, spooned and leveled

1 teaspoon baking soda

1 teaspoon ground ginger

1 teaspoon ground cinnamon

½ teaspoon kosher salt

⅛ teaspoon ground nutmeg

Pinch of ground cloves

1¼ cups [250 g] granulated sugar

½ cup [100 g] light brown sugar, packed

½ cup [113 g] unsalted butter, room temperature

2 tablespoons molasses (not blackstrap)

1 egg, at room temperature

1 teaspoon vanilla extract

SNICKERDOODLE AND CHOCOLATE COOKIES

2¼ cups [280 g] all-purpose flour, spooned and leveled

1 teaspoon baking soda

1 teaspoon cream of tartar

½ teaspoon kosher salt

1¼ cups [250 g] granulated sugar

½ cup [100 g] light brown sugar, packed

½ cup [113 g] unsalted butter, at room temperature

1 egg, at room temperature

1 teaspoon vanilla extract

2 tablespoons Dutch-process cocoa powder, sifted

FOR ASSEMBLY

1 recipe Cinnamon Buttercream (page 249)

Flaky salt, for sprinkling (optional)

Snickerdoodles are great on their own, but pair them with a warmly spiced ginger cookie and a rich chocolate sugar cookie, and you have yourself the MVP award for the coziest cookie ever. They're basically three cookies in one, and everyone I feed them to loves them. The cookies bake up very soft, then firm up after a few minutes of cooling, so don't be tempted to overbake them.

TO MAKE THE TOPPING
Combine the granulated sugar, cinnamon, and salt in a small bowl. Set aside.

TO MAKE THE GINGER COOKIES
Adjust the oven rack to the middle position and preheat the oven to 350°F [180°C]. Line two baking sheets with parchment paper or silicone baking mats.

cont.

In a medium bowl, whisk together the flour, baking soda, ginger, cinnamon, salt, nutmeg, and cloves.

In the bowl of a stand mixer fitted with the paddle attachment, beat the granulated sugar, brown sugar, and butter on medium-low speed for about 2 minutes. Stop the mixer and scrape down the sides of the bowl as needed. Add the molasses and mix for another 30 seconds. Add the egg and mix until combined. Add the vanilla and mix until incorporated. Slowly add the flour mixture and mix on low speed for about 30 seconds, until the dough comes together.

Scoop 1 tablespoon of dough at a time and roll into a ball. Place the dough balls on a prepared baking sheet and refrigerate while you make the snickerdoodle dough.

TO MAKE THE SNICKERDOODLE AND CHOCOLATE COOKIES
In a medium bowl, whisk together the flour, baking soda, cream of tartar, and salt.

In the bowl of a stand mixer fitted with the paddle attachment, beat the granulated sugar, brown sugar, and butter for about 2 minutes. Stop the mixer and scrape down the sides of the bowl as needed. Add the egg and vanilla and mix on low for about 30 seconds, until combined. Add the flour mixture and mix on low speed for about 30 seconds, until the dough comes together. Remove half of the dough from the bowl and add the cocoa powder to the half in the stand mixer. Mix to combine.

Scoop ½ tablespoon of the snickerdoodle dough, roll into a ball, and place it on the second prepared baking sheet. Repeat with all the snickerdoodle dough, and then all the chocolate dough.

Take one ball of ginger cookie dough, one ball of snickerdoodle dough, and one ball of chocolate snickerdoodle dough and smoosh them together, rolling into a larger ball of dough.

Generously coat the ball of dough in the cinnamon sugar mix and place on a prepared baking sheet. Using the palm of your hand, gently flatten the cookie into a disk shape. Repeat with the remaining cookie dough.

Bake the cookies for 10 to 11 minutes, or until the edges are set. Remove from the oven and let cool for 10 minutes on the baking sheet before using a spatula to carefully transfer the cookies to a wire cooling rack. Let cool completely before adding the filling.

TO ASSEMBLE THE COOKIE SANDWICHES

Transfer the Cinnamon Buttercream to a piping bag fitted with a large tip. Flip half of the cookies over so they're flat-side up. Pipe about 2 tablespoons of buttercream onto the flat side of each cookie. Top each with a second cookie, flat-side down, and gently press together to form a sandwich. Sprinkle the tops of the cookie sandwiches with flaky salt, if desired.

Store the cookie sandwiches tightly wrapped at room temperature for up to 3 days.

GINGERBREAD COOKIES
WITH
PUMPKIN SPICE BUTTERCREAM

GINGERBREAD COOKIES

3½ cups [440 g] all-purpose flour, spooned and leveled

¼ cup [35 g] cornstarch

2 teaspoons ground cinnamon

2 teaspoons ground ginger

½ teaspoon salt

¼ teaspoon ground cloves

1 cup [200 g] dark brown sugar, packed

¾ cup [170 g] unsalted butter, at room temperature

⅔ cup [210 g] molasses (not blackstrap)

1 egg, at room temperature

1 teaspoon vanilla extract

FOR ASSEMBLY

1 recipe Pumpkin Spice Buttercream (page 253)

Spiced cookies are an enduring holiday tradition that never gets old. But these are not your grandmother's gingerbread cookies. They roll out like a dream and bake up soft and chewy, not dry and crumbly. They're warmly spiced and bold with molasses. Any extra dough can be squirreled away in the freezer to bake up when you feel like having Christmas in July.

TO MAKE THE COOKIES

In a medium bowl, whisk together the flour, cornstarch, cinnamon, ginger, salt, and cloves.

In the bowl of a stand mixer fitted with the paddle attachment, mix together the brown sugar and butter. Mix together on medium speed until light and fluffy, about 2 minutes. Stop the mixer and scrape down the sides of the bowl. Add the molasses and mix on medium-low speed until well combined. Add the egg and vanilla, mixing to combine. Scrape down the sides of the bowl once more. Add the flour mixture in two additions, mixing on low speed after each to combine. Stop the mixer when only a few streaks of flour remain.

Remove the bowl from the mixer and use a sturdy spatula or wooden spoon to turn the dough once or twice more until the flour is incorporated.

cont.

Transfer the dough to your work surface and divide it in half. Wrap one half in plastic wrap and set aside. Use a rolling pin to roll the other half of the dough between two large pieces of parchment paper until it is about ¼ in [6 mm] thick. (To keep the parchment paper from sliding on the counter-top, place it on top of a silicone baking mat.) Repeat with the second half of the dough. Stack the parchment-lined dough slabs one on top of the other on a baking sheet and refrigerate for 2 hours.

Once the dough is chilled (it should be firm to the touch), preheat the oven to 350°F [180°C]. Line two baking sheets with parchment paper or silicone baking mats.

Remove the top sheet of parchment paper from the dough and use a medium cookie cutter or cookie stamp to cut out shapes. You can use a classic gingerbread man shape or anything that feels holiday-ish to you. Cut the cookies as close to each other as possible so as not to waste any dough. Use your hands or a metal spatula to transfer the dough to the prepared baking sheets. Gather any scraps and reroll the dough while it is still cold. Continue cutting shapes until all the dough is used. If the dough gets too warm at any time, roll it flat and return it to the refrigerator to chill.

Bake the cookies for 8 to 9 minutes, or until the edges are set but the centers are still soft. Do not overbake. Remove the cookies from the oven and allow them to cool on the baking sheet for 4 to 5 minutes before using a spatula to carefully transfer them to a wire cooling rack to cool completely.

To keep the dough cold as long as possible, bake the first sheet of cookies before beginning the steps of cutting and rerolling with the second piece of dough. Continue until all the dough has been used.

TO ASSEMBLE THE COOKIE SANDWICHES
Transfer the Pumpkin Spice Buttercream to a piping bag fitted with a large tip. Flip half of the cookies over so they're flat-side up. Pipe about 2 tablespoons of buttercream onto the flat side of each cookie. Top each with a second cookie, flat-side down, and gently press together to form a sandwich.

Store the cookie sandwiches tightly covered at room temperature for up to 4 days.

CHAI SHORTBREAD
WITH
MAPLE BROWN BUTTER FROSTING

I'm a sucker for chai spice in general, but when you add a spiced sugar sprinkle and maple brown butter frosting, there's no topping that. This shortbread is subtler in flavor than most, with a delicate carnival of textures that will win over the most discriminating of palates. If you're still on the fence about chai, give these a go. You won't be sorry.

CHAI SUGAR TOPPING

⅓ cup [65 g] granulated sugar

1½ teaspoons ground cinnamon

½ teaspoon ground ginger

¼ teaspoon ground allspice

¼ teaspoon ground cardamom

⅛ teaspoon ground cloves

CHAI SHORTBREAD

¾ cup [170 g] unsalted butter, at room temperature

¾ cup [150 g] light brown sugar, packed

1 egg, at room temperature

2 teaspoons vanilla extract

3 cups [375 g] all-purpose flour, spooned and leveled

¾ teaspoon ground cinnamon

½ teaspoon baking soda

½ teaspoon salt

¼ teaspoon ground ginger

¼ teaspoon ground cardamom

⅛ teaspoon ground nutmeg

⅛ teaspoon ground allspice

FOR ASSEMBLY

1 recipe Maple Brown Butter Frosting (page 256)

TO MAKE THE TOPPING
In a small bowl, combine the granulated sugar, cinnamon, ginger, allspice, cardamom, and cloves. Set aside.

TO MAKE THE SHORTBREAD
In the bowl of a stand mixer fitted with the paddle attachment, combine the butter and brown sugar. Beat the mixture until light and fluffy, 4 to 5 minutes. Add the egg, followed by the vanilla. Mix to combine well and then stop the mixer and scrape down the sides of the bowl. Add the flour, cinnamon, baking soda, salt, ginger, cardamom, nutmeg, and allspice. Beat on low speed until the mixture begins to come together and form a ball.

Transfer the dough to your work surface and divide it in half. Wrap one half with plastic wrap and set aside. Use a rolling pin to roll the other half of the dough between two large pieces of parchment paper until it is about ¼ in [6 mm] thick. (To keep the parchment paper from sliding on the countertop, place it on top of a silicone baking mat.) Repeat with the second half of the dough. Stack the parchment-lined dough slabs one on top of the other on a baking sheet and refrigerate for at least 2 hours.

cont.

Once the dough is chilled, preheat the oven to 350°F [180°C]. Line two baking sheets with parchment paper or silicone baking mats.

Use a 2 in [5 cm] circle cookie cutter (or a leaf cookie cutter would also be fun) to cut shapes from the chilled dough. Transfer the dough pieces to the prepared baking sheets 1 in [2.5 cm] apart; the dough will not spread while baking.

Roll out the leftover scraps of dough between two sheets of parchment paper and continue cutting cookies until all the dough has been used. If the dough becomes too soft, chill again before cutting the remaining shapes.

Bake for 8 to 9 minutes, or until the edges just begin to brown. Do not overbake. Remove the cookies from the oven and immediately dust the tops generously with the Chai Sugar Topping. Use a spatula to carefully transfer the cookies to a wire cooling rack and let cool completely before assembling the cookie sandwiches.

TO ASSEMBLE THE COOKIE SANDWICHES
Use a spoon or piping bag to place about 2 teaspoons of Maple Brown Butter Frosting on the flat side of a cookie. Top with a second cookie, flat-side down, and gently press together to form a sandwich. Repeat with the remaining cookies and frosting.

Store the cookie sandwiches tightly covered at room temperature for up to 3 days.

PUMPKIN SPICE SUGAR COOKIES
WITH
BROWN BUTTER CREAM CHEESE FROSTING

CINNAMON SUGAR TOPPING

2 tablespoons dark brown sugar, packed

1 tablespoon granulated sugar

½ teaspoon ground cinnamon

Pinch of ground nutmeg

PUMPKIN SPICE SUGAR COOKIES

2 cups plus 2 tablespoons [265 g] all-purpose flour, spooned and leveled

1 teaspoon baking soda

1 teaspoon ground cinnamon

½ teaspoon baking powder

½ teaspoon kosher salt

¼ teaspoon ground nutmeg

¼ teaspoon ground ginger

⅛ teaspoon ground cloves

1 cup [226 g] unsalted butter

1 cup [200 g] dark brown sugar, packed

¼ cup [50 g] granulated sugar

⅓ cup [80 g] pumpkin purée (not pumpkin pie filling)

1 egg yolk, at room temperature

1 tablespoon molasses (not blackstrap)

1½ teaspoons vanilla extract

FOR ASSEMBLY

1 recipe Brown Butter Cream Cheese Frosting (page 257)

If I had to pick a favorite cookie sandwich in this book, this would be it. (Sshhh . . . don't tell chocolate.) As soon as the calendar strikes September 1, these spiced pumpkin cookies are on heavy repeat in my kitchen. You might be surprised to learn that I don't like pumpkin pie (can we still be friends?). But I loooovee these soft and chewy pumpkin cookies with the perfect blend of spices to keep things interesting. Don't skip the brown butter cream cheese frosting—there is no other way.

TO MAKE THE TOPPING

In a small bowl, whisk together the brown sugar, granulated sugar, cinnamon, and nutmeg. Set aside.

TO MAKE THE COOKIES

In a medium bowl, whisk together the flour, baking soda, cinnamon, baking powder, salt, nutmeg, ginger, and cloves. Set aside.

Melt the butter in a medium saucepan over medium-high heat. Once it has melted, begin stirring often and stay close to the stove top. The butter will crackle and pop as it browns and it will start to foam slightly. Once the sizzling sound stops, continue stirring constantly until golden-brown bits begin to collect on the bottom of the pan. The butter will smell slightly nutty and be amber in color.

cont.

Remove from the heat and pour the butter into a heatproof bowl, making sure to scrape all the brown butter solids from the bottom of the pan. Chill in the refrigerator for about 25 minutes. Do not let it solidify.

Once the butter has chilled, preheat the oven to 350°F [180°C]. Line two baking sheets with parchment paper or silicone baking mats.

Add the chilled brown butter to the bowl of a stand mixer fitted with the paddle attachment. Add the brown sugar and granulated sugar and mix to combine, about 1 minute. The mixture will resemble wet sand. Add the pumpkin, egg yolk, molasses, and vanilla. Mix on low speed until well combined. Stop the mixer and scrape down the sides of the bowl. Add the flour mixture and mix until combined. Do not overmix. The dough will be very soft but not sticky.

Use a 3 tablespoon cookie scoop to scoop the dough. Do not roll the cookie into a ball. Drop each cookie into the cinnamon sugar mixture and toss to coat while keeping the scooped form of the cookie intact.

Place the coated cookies on the prepared baking sheets, leaving 3 in [7.5 cm] between to allow for spreading. Bake for 10 to 12 minutes, or until the cookies are set on the edges and still puffed up in the center. The cookies will deflate as they cool.

Remove the cookies from the oven and let them cool on the baking sheets for 10 minutes before using a spatula to carefully transfer the cookies to a wire cooling rack to cool completely before assembling the cookie sandwiches.

TO ASSEMBLE THE COOKIE SANDWICHES
Use a spoon or piping bag fitted with a star tip to place a generous swirl of Brown Butter Cream Cheese Frosting on the flat side of a cookie. Top with a second cookie, flat-side down, and gently press the cookies together to form a sandwich. Repeat with the remaining cookies and buttercream.

Store the cookies tightly covered at room temperature for up to 3 days. Once assembled, store the cookie sandwiches in the refrigerator for up to 3 days. For softer cookies, leave out at room temperature for 20 minutes before serving.

COCKTAIL COOKIES

ROSEMARY PINE NUT SABLÉS
WITH
WHIPPED GOAT CHEESE

ROSEMARY PINE NUT SABLÉS

1 tablespoon fresh rosemary, coarsely chopped

½ cup [60 g] pine nuts, toasted and cooled

1¼ cups [155 g] all-purpose flour, spooned and leveled

2 tablespoons sugar

1 teaspoon fine sea salt

7 tablespoons [100 g] unsalted butter, cubed and cold

1 egg, at room temperature

FOR ASSEMBLY

1 recipe Whipped Goat Cheese Filling (page 260)

Kick your cheese and cracker game up a notch with these savory sablés filled with a tangy goat cheese filling. Bursting with rich, buttery flavor, these sablés are deceptively easy to whip up. Use the highest-quality butter you can get your hands on for the very best flavor.

TO MAKE THE SABLÉS
Place the rosemary and pine nuts into a food processor fitted with the blade attachment and pulse until the pine nuts are coarsely chopped. Add the flour, sugar, and salt and pulse until everything is combined. Add the cold butter and pulse until the butter is in pea-size (or smaller) bits and evenly distributed. Add the egg and pulse until the dough starts to come together.

Transfer the dough to the middle of a 15 in [38 cm] strip of plastic wrap. Use the plastic wrap to roll the dough into a 12 in [30.5 cm] log that is about 1½ to 2 in [4 to 5 cm] in diameter. Wrap the log of dough tightly in the plastic wrap and place in the freezer for 1 hour.

When the dough log is almost done chilling adjust the oven rack to the middle position and preheat the oven to 350°F [180°C]. Line two baking sheets with parchment paper or silicone baking mats.

cont.

Remove the dough from the freezer, unwrap, and, using a sharp knife, slice ¼ in [6 mm] thick sablés. Slightly rotate the log after each slice to keep the shape consistently round. Place the slices on the prepared baking sheets, 1 in [2.5 cm] apart. If the sablés are starting to squish and lose their round shape when being cut, place the log back in the freezer.

Bake the sablés for 10 to 12 minutes, or until the edges just start to turn golden. Remove from the oven and let cool on the baking sheets for 5 minutes before using a spatula to carefully transfer them to a wire cooling rack. Let cool completely before adding the filling.

TO ASSEMBLE THE SABLÉ SANDWICHES
Line up half of the baked sablés and flip them over so they're flat-side up. Add a dollop of the Whipped Goat Cheese Filling to the upside-down sablés. Top each with a second sablé, flat-side down, and gently press together to form a sandwich.

Serve right away, or store the sablé sandwiches tightly covered in the refrigerator for up to 3 days.

LEMON THYME SHORTBREAD
WITH
WHIPPED MASCARPONE FILLING

LEMON THYME SHORTBREAD

1½ cups [190 g] all-purpose flour, spooned and leveled

¼ cup [35 g] cornstarch

1 teaspoon fine sea salt

¼ cup [50 g] granulated sugar

1 tablespoon finely chopped fresh thyme

1 tablespoon lemon zest, from one large lemon

½ cup [113 g] unsalted butter, at room temperature

2 tablespoons fresh lemon juice

1 egg yolk, at room temperature

FOR ASSEMBLY

1 recipe Whipped Mascarpone Filling (page 259)

Shortbread is one of my favorite things to bake. While I tend to go the sweet route, every now and then I crave a savory shortbread, and these lemon and thyme crackers are my go-to. Bake them as directed for a soft shortbread or roll them thinner and leave in the oven for an extra minute or two for a crisper texture. Enjoy these on the porch with your favorite chilled wine or whatever you like to drink at cocktail hour.

TO MAKE THE SHORTBREAD
Adjust the oven rack to the middle position and preheat the oven to 350°F [180°C]. Line two baking sheets with parchment paper or silicone baking mats.

In a medium bowl, whisk together the flour, cornstarch, and salt.

In a small bowl, combine the sugar, thyme, and lemon zest and rub the ingredients together with your fingers to release the oils from the lemon zest. Add this mixture, as well as the butter and lemon juice, to a food processor fitted with the blade attachment and pulse a couple of times until smooth. Add the egg yolk and pulse several more times. Add the flour mixture and pulse until the dough just starts to come together.

cont.

Transfer the dough to a piece of parchment paper and form a flattened disk with your hands. Place another piece of parchment paper on top of the dough and, using a rolling pin, roll out the dough to ¼ in [6 mm] thick. Use a 2 in [5 cm] round cookie cutter to cut out the cookie shape. Transfer the cookies to a prepared baking sheet, 1 to 2 in [2.5 to 5 cm] apart.

Combine the leftover dough into a flattened disk, roll it out between two pieces of parchment paper, and place in the freezer while the other cookies are baking. This will keep the dough chilled and make cutting the remaining shapes easier.

Bake for 15 to 17 minutes, or until the edges of the shortbread begin to turn golden brown. Remove from the oven and let cool on the baking sheet for 5 minutes before using a spatula to carefully transfer the shortbread to a wire cooling rack to cool completely before adding the filling. Repeat with the remaining dough until all the shortbread is baked.

TO ASSEMBLE THE SHORTBREAD SANDWICHES
Line up half of the baked shortbread and flip them over so they're flat-side up. Add about 1 tablespoon of the Whipped Mascarpone Filling to the top of each shortbread. Top each with a second shortbread, flat-side down, and gently press together to form a sandwich.

The shortbread (without filling) will stay fresh tightly covered at room temperature for 5 days. Once assembled, the sandwiches are best enjoyed the day they are made and should be refrigerated.

PARMESAN PIZZELLE
WITH
WHIPPED HERB CREAM CHEESE

PIZZELLE

1¼ cups [155 g] all-purpose flour, spooned and leveled

½ cup [50 g] finely grated Parmesan cheese, lightly packed

1 tablespoon granulated sugar

2 teaspoons baking powder

1 teaspoon salt

¼ teaspoon garlic powder

4 eggs, at room temperature

½ cup [113 g] unsalted butter, melted and cooled

FOR ASSEMBLY

1 recipe Whipped Herb Cream Cheese (page 260)

Pizzelle are traditional Italian cookies, often served sweet with a dusting of confectioners' sugar. They can be made only in a special pizzelle iron, which cooks the thick, egg-laden dough into a crisp, buttery wafer. It's a thing of magic. For this savory version, use the best Parmesan you can find and don't skimp on the herbs in the whipped cream cheese. Pizzelle are best eaten the day they are made, but you can crisp them up easily with a short stint in the oven.

TO MAKE THE PIZZELLE
Plug in the pizzelle iron and grease and preheat on the highest setting according to the manufacturer's directions.

In a medium bowl, whisk together the flour, Parmesan, sugar, baking powder, salt, and garlic powder.

In a large bowl, whisk the eggs. Add the melted cooled butter and whisk to combine well. Add the dry ingredients and fold with a spatula until there are no longer any streaks of flour.

Once the pizzelle iron is heated, place about 1 tablespoon of batter just slightly off center toward the back of the iron. Close the iron and cook for 75 to 90 seconds, or until the steam stops and the pizzella turns golden brown. Carefully remove with an offset spatula and transfer to a wire cooling rack to cool completely before adding the filling. Repeat until all the batter is used.

cont.

TO ASSEMBLE THE PIZZELLE SANDWICHES

Once the pizzelle have cooled, use an offset spatula to add 2 tablespoons of the Whipped Herb Cream Cheese to half of the pizzelle. Top each with a second pizzella and gently press together to create a sandwich.

Pizzelle are best enjoyed on the same day they are made. Store in an airtight container at room temperature and wait to assemble until ready to serve.

EVERYTHING BAGEL CRACKERS
WITH
CHIVE CREAM CHEESE

EVERYTHING BAGEL CRACKERS

2 cups [250 g] all-purpose flour, spooned and leveled

½ cup [50 g] finely grated Parmesan cheese

¾ teaspoon salt

¾ cup [170 g] unsalted butter, at room temperature and cubed

1 egg, at room temperature

1 tablespoon heavy cream

¼ cup [40 g] everything bagel seasoning blend (see Note)

FOR ASSEMBLY

1 recipe Chive Cream Cheese Filling (page 260)

Trader Joe's Everything but the Bagel seasoning is like magic fairy dust in our house. We sprinkle it on everything from avocado toast to scrambled eggs and homemade buttermilk biscuits. These bite-size everything bagel crackers won't last 5 minutes on the kitchen counter, whether you serve them as a dinner party hors d'oeuvre or an after-school snack. They're proof that you can never have too much of a good thing.

TO MAKE THE CRACKERS
In the bowl of a food processor fitted with the blade attachment, combine the flour, Parmesan, and salt. Pulse a few times to mix. Add the butter and pulse until the dough comes together.

Lay a 12 in [30.5 cm] piece of plastic wrap on your work surface. Transfer the dough to the middle of the plastic wrap. Wrap the dough in the plastic wrap, using the wrap to press the dough into a flat disk shape. Place the tightly wrapped disk of dough in the refrigerator for 1 hour, until firm.

While the dough is chilling, whisk together the egg and heavy cream in a small bowl. Set aside.

Adjust the oven rack to the middle position and preheat the oven to 350°F [180°C]. Line two baking sheets with parchment paper or silicone baking mats. Set aside.

cont.

NOTE

You can use Trader Joe's
Everything but the Bagel
Sesame seasoning here, or
you can easily make your own.
Combine 1 tablespoon white
sesame seeds, 2 teaspoons
black sesame seeds, 2 teaspoons dried minced onion,
2 teaspoons dried minced
garlic, 1½ teaspoons poppy
seeds, and 1 teaspoon flaky
sea salt such as Maldon.

Once the dough is chilled, lightly flour your work surface and a rolling pin. Roll out the dough to ¼ in [6 mm] thick. Use a 2 in [5 cm] square cookie cutter or a knife to cut out square shapes.

Place the crackers, spaced 1 to 2 in [2.5 to 5 cm] apart, on a prepared baking sheet. Brush the cracker tops with the egg wash and sprinkle generously with everything bagel seasoning. Use a fork or toothpick to prick each cracker a few times.

After you have rolled out the dough for the first time and cut out as many crackers as possible, combine the scraps and form another flat disk. Wrap the disk in the plastic wrap and place in the refrigerator again for 15 minutes while the first batch bakes.

Bake for 12 to 13 minutes, or until the edges are just starting to turn golden brown.

Remove the crackers from the oven and let cool for 5 min-utes on the baking sheet before using a spatula to carefully transfer the crackers to a wire cooling rack to cool com-pletely before adding the filling.

Repeat until all the dough has been rolled out, cut, and baked.

TO ASSEMBLE THE CRACKER SANDWICHES

Once the crackers have cooled, use a piping bag or a tea-spoon to add 1 to 2 teaspoons of the Chive Cream Cheese Filling to the bottom side of half the crackers. Top each with another cracker and gently press together to form a sandwich.

Sprinkle with more everything bagel seasoning, if desired. The cracker sandwiches will stay fresh for up to 3 days but are best eaten the day they are assembled.

PARMESAN POLENTA CRACKERS
WITH
CHIVE CREAM CHEESE

PARMESAN POLENTA CRACKERS

1½ cups [190 g] all-purpose flour, spooned and leveled

¾ cup [105 g] finely ground yellow cornmeal

2 teaspoons fine sea salt

¼ teaspoon freshly ground black pepper

6 tablespoons [85 g] unsalted butter, cold and cubed

¼ cup plus 2 tablespoons [35 g] finely grated Parmesan cheese

½ cup [120 ml] heavy cream

1 tablespoon ice-cold water, as needed

FOR ASSEMBLY

1 recipe Chive Cream Cheese Filling (page 260)

These crisp, savory crackers come together easily in a food processor and are delicious served with a schmear of chive cream cheese. For perfectly crispy crackers, don't forget to poke holes in the crackers before baking. Pile them on a platter as an appetizer or pack them in your lunch box. No matter how you serve them, I betcha can't have just one!

TO MAKE THE CRACKERS
Adjust the oven rack to the middle position and preheat the oven to 350°F [180°C]. Line two baking sheets with parchment paper or silicone baking mats.

In the bowl of a food processor fitted with the blade attachment, combine the flour, cornmeal, salt, and pepper and pulse to mix. Add the butter and Parmesan and pulse until the butter is in pea-size bits. Add the heavy cream and pulse until the dough just starts to pull away from the sides of the bowl and form a ball. If the dough does not come together, add 1 tablespoon of ice-cold water and pulse until combined.

Transfer the dough to a large piece of parchment paper on your work surface and form the dough into a disk shape. Place the dough in the refrigerator and let chill for 15 minutes while the oven continues to preheat.

cont.

Remove the dough from the refrigerator and add another piece of parchment paper on top. Using a rolling pin, roll out the dough to a thickness between ⅛ and ¼ in [3 to 6 mm]. Use a 2 in [5 cm] square cookie cutter to cut out the crackers. Place the crackers, spaced 1 to 2 in [2.5 to 5 cm] apart, on the prepared baking sheets. Prick the squares three or four times each with a fork.

Gather the scraps and combine the leftover dough into a flattened disk, roll out between parchment, and place in the freezer to keep cold while the first batch of crackers is baking. This will make cutting out the remaining shapes easier.

Bake the crackers for 9 to 12 minutes, or until the edges just start to turn golden brown. Remove from the oven and let cool on the baking sheet for 5 minutes before using a spatula to carefully transfer the crackers to a wire cooling rack to cool completely before assembling the sandwiches.

Continue to roll out and bake until all the remaining dough has been used. You should end up with about 36 crackers.

TO ASSEMBLE THE CRACKER SANDWICHES
Line up half of the baked crackers and flip them over so they're flat-side up. Add about 1 tablespoon of the Chive Cream Cheese Filling to each of the flipped-over crackers. Top each with a second cracker, flat-side down, and gently press together to create a sandwich.

These are best enjoyed the day they are made.

CORNBREAD COOKIES
WITH
HONEY MASCARPONE

CORNBREAD COOKIES

¾ cup [105 g] yellow cornmeal

1¼ cups [155 g] all-purpose flour, spooned and leveled

½ teaspoon baking soda

¼ teaspoon baking powder

½ cup [113 g] salted butter, at room temperature

1 tablespoon coconut oil, soft but not melted

⅓ cup [65 g] granulated sugar

¼ cup [50 g] light brown sugar, packed

1 egg, at room temperature

1 tablespoon honey

1 teaspoon vanilla extract

FOR ASSEMBLY

1 recipe Honey Mascarpone (page 259)

This recipe crams all the beloved flavors of warm buttery cornbread into perfectly sweet and savory cookies that are best devoured straight from the oven. I like to finish them off with a drizzle of local honey for a stress-free party snack that's as easy as it is delicious.

TO MAKE THE COOKIES

Adjust the oven rack to the middle position and preheat the oven to 350°F [180°C]. Line two baking sheets with parchment paper or silicone baking mats.

In the bowl of a food processor fitted with the blade attachment, pulse the cornmeal three to four times to make the granules less coarse.

In a medium bowl, whisk together the cornmeal, flour, baking soda, and baking powder. Set aside.

In the bowl of a stand mixer fitted with the paddle attachment, beat together the butter, coconut oil, granulated sugar, and brown sugar on medium speed for 2 minutes, until light and fluffy. Stop the mixer and scrape down the sides of the bowl as needed. Add the egg, honey, and vanilla. Mix to combine. Add the flour mixture and mix on low speed for about 30 seconds until fully incorporated.

Use a 2 tablespoon cookie scoop to portion the dough onto the prepared baking sheets 2 in [5 cm] apart.

cont.

Bake the cookies for 8 to 9 minutes, or until the edges are set but the centers are still soft. Do not overbake. Remove the cookies from the oven and let cool on the baking sheet for 4 to 5 minutes before using a spatula to carefully transfer them to a wire cooling rack to cool completely.

TO ASSEMBLE THE COOKIE SANDWICHES
Flip half of the cookies over so they're flat-side up. Spread about 1 tablespoon of Honey Mascarpone onto the flat side of one cookie. Top with a second cookie, flat-side down, and gently press together to form a sandwich. Repeat with the remaining cookies and Honey Mascarpone.

Store the cookies (without filling) tightly covered at room temperature for up to 3 days. Once assembled, the cookie sandwiches should be enjoyed the day they are made and stored in the refrigerator.

BLUE CHEESE AND WALNUT SLICE 'N' BAKES
WITH
FIG PRESERVES

BLUE CHEESE AND WALNUT CRACKERS

1¼ cups [155 g] all-purpose flour, spooned and leveled

2 tablespoons granulated sugar

1 teaspoon finely chopped fresh rosemary

1 teaspoon kosher salt

⅛ teaspoon freshly cracked black pepper

¾ cup [90 g] crumbled blue cheese

½ cup [60 g] chopped walnuts, lightly toasted and cooled

7 tablespoons [100 g] unsalted butter, cold and cubed

1 egg

1 tablespoon ice-cold water, as needed

FOR ASSEMBLY

⅓ cup [100 g] store-bought fig preserves

Don't be overwhelmed by the amount of blue cheese in these crackers. It's just right, I promise (unless of course you don't like blue cheese, in which case you probably shouldn't be making this cracker). Do try to chill the dough the full 3 hours and reach for your sharpest knife when it comes time to slice. If the dough crumbles a bit, not to worry. Just patch the pieces back together and bake away. They'll still be delicious!

TO MAKE THE CRACKERS
In the bowl of a food processor fitted with the blade attachment, pulse together the flour, sugar, rosemary, salt, and pepper until combined. Add the blue cheese and walnuts, pulsing three or four times until incorporated.

Add the cold butter and continue pulsing until the butter is in pea-size bits and the mixture just begins to come together. Add the egg and pulse several more times until the dough comes together in a ball. If the dough is still too dry, add 1 tablespoon cold water and pulse to combine well.

Transfer the dough to a large piece of plastic wrap and form into a log about 10 in [25 cm] long. Use your hands to roll and shape it. Wrap it in the plastic wrap and refrigerate for at least 3 hours.

When the dough is fully chilled, preheat the oven to 375°F [190°C] and line two baking sheets with parchment paper or silicone baking mats.

cont.

Remove the dough from the refrigerator and unwrap the plastic. Use a sharp knife to cut ¼ in [6 mm] slices from the log and place them on the prepared baking sheets, leaving ½ to 1 in [13 mm to 2.5 cm] between each cracker. Chill the remaining dough in the refrigerator while the cookies bake.

Bake for 12 to 13 minutes, or until the edges are golden brown and the centers are set. Rotate the pans halfway through baking.

Remove the crackers from the oven and let cool on the baking sheets for 15 minutes before using a spatula to carefully transfer them to a wire cooling rack to cool completely. Repeat with the remaining dough.

TO ASSEMBLE THE CRACKER SANDWICHES
Spoon 1 teaspoon of fig preserves onto the flat side of one cracker and top with a second cracker, flat-side down. Gently press together to form a sandwich. Repeat with the remaining crackers and preserves.

The cracker sandwiches are best enjoyed the day they are made. Store any leftover crackers without preserves, tightly covered at room temperature for up to 3 days.

THE FILLINGS

DULCE DE LECHE

MAKES 2½ CUPS [795 G]

Two 14 oz [400 g] cans sweetened condensed milk

Pinch of fine sea salt

Adjust the oven rack to the middle position and preheat the oven to 425°F [220°C].

Pour the condensed milk into a pie plate and sprinkle with salt. Cover the pie plate with aluminum foil and place in a deeper baking dish that is filled halfway up the pie plate with hot water.

Place in the preheated oven for 2 to 2½ hours. Check every 15 to 20 minutes to make sure water remains in the baking dish. Add more as needed.

Remove the baking dish from the oven when the dulce de leche has darkened to a golden amber color. Allow to cool to room temperature before whisking smooth.

Transfer to a piping bag fitted with a round tip to use right away, or store tightly covered in the refrigerator for up to 2 weeks.

SALTED CARAMEL

MAKES 1 CUP [230 G]

¾ cup [150 g] granulated sugar

4 tablespoons [55 g] unsalted butter, at room temperature

¼ cup [60 ml] heavy cream, at room temperature

1 teaspoon vanilla extract

¼ teaspoon kosher salt

In a small heavy-bottomed pot over medium-low heat, melt the sugar, whisking occasionally. The sugar will clump up and turn a darker color as it cooks. Once the sugar is completely melted and has turned a dark amber color, add the butter and whisk to combine. The mixture will crackle and pop.

Continue stirring until all the butter is melted. Let the mixture simmer for 1 minute without stirring. Turn the heat to low and slowly add the heavy cream, stirring constantly. Once all the cream has been added, increase the heat to medium and bring the mixture to a boil. Boil for 1 minute.

Remove from the heat and add the vanilla and salt, whisking to combine.

Pour the caramel into a heatproof bowl or jar and rest at room temperature for 15 minutes. Place in the refrigerator to cool completely. The caramel will thicken as it cools.

Use immediately or store tightly covered in the refrigerator for up to 1 month.

SALTED CARAMEL BUTTERCREAM

MAKES 4 CUPS [800 G]

1 cup [226 g] unsalted butter, at room temperature

4 cups [480 g] confectioners' sugar, sifted

¼ cup [58 g] Salted Caramel (above) or store-bought, at room temperature

Pinch of salt

1 to 2 tablespoons heavy cream or whole milk

In the bowl of a stand mixer fitted with the paddle attachment, beat the butter on medium speed for 1 minute until light and creamy. Stop the mixer and scrape down the sides of the bowl. Slowly add the confectioners' sugar, 1 cup [120 g] at a time, mixing on low speed after each addition until combined. Increase the speed to medium-high and mix for 1 minute. Scrape down the sides of the bowl once more and add the salted caramel and salt. Mix on low speed to combine and then increase the speed to medium-high, mixing until light and fluffy. Add 1 tablespoon of the heavy cream. Mix for 1 minute on medium-high speed until light and airy. If the buttercream is too thick, add more heavy cream.

Use immediately or store tightly covered in the refrigerator for up to 2 weeks.

CHOCOLATE GANACHE

MAKES ⅔ CUP [170 G]

4 oz [115 g] chocolate, finely chopped (see Note)

⅓ cup [80 ml] heavy cream

Place the chopped chocolate in a heatproof bowl.

In a small saucepan over medium-low heat, heat the heavy cream until simmering. Do not let it boil. Pour the hot cream over the chocolate and let sit for 4 to 5 minutes. Whisk until smooth and shiny. Allow to sit at room temperature for about 30 minutes to thicken to a spreadable consistency.

Use immediately or store tightly covered in the refrigerator for up to 2 weeks.

Note: For this recipe, you can use bittersweet, milk, or white chocolate.

VARIATIONS

MINT CHOCOLATE GANACHE

Add ⅛ teaspoon mint extract to the bowl of hot cream and chocolate before mixing smooth. Note that extracts vary in strength, so adjust to taste.

ORANGE CHOCOLATE GANACHE

Add the zest of one orange to the bowl of hot cream and chocolate before mixing smooth.

WHIPPED NUTELLA GANACHE

MAKES 3 CUPS [500 G]

1 cup [140 g] coarsely chopped dark chocolate

1 cup [240 ml] heavy cream

⅔ cup [210 g] Nutella or other hazelnut spread, at room temperature

Place the chopped chocolate in a heatproof bowl. In a small saucepan over medium-low heat, heat the heavy cream until just simmering. Do not let it boil.

Pour the hot cream over the chopped chocolate and let sit for 5 minutes. Add the Nutella and whisk to combine.

Allow to cool to room temperature, stirring occasionally. At this point, you may place the ganache in the refrigerator to speed this along.

Once cooled, transfer the ganache to the bowl of a stand mixer fitted with the paddle attachment and whip on high speed until light and fluffy, 2 to 3 minutes. It will lighten in color and the whipped ganache should hold its form.

Use immediately or store tightly covered in the refrigerator for up to 2 weeks.

VANILLA BUTTERCREAM

MAKES 3¼ CUPS [540 G]

½ cup [113 g] unsalted butter, at room temperature

2 teaspoons vanilla extract

¼ teaspoon salt

3½ cups [420 g] confectioners' sugar, sifted, plus more as needed

1 to 2 tablespoons heavy cream or whole milk

In the bowl of a stand mixer fitted with the paddle attachment, beat the butter for 1 minute, until light and creamy. Stop the mixer and scrape down the sides of the bowl. Add the vanilla and salt, mixing to combine. Add the confectioners' sugar, 1 cup [120 g] at a time while mixing on low speed. Once the sugar is incorporated, add 1 tablespoon of the heavy cream, increase the speed to medium-high, and mix for 2 to 3 minutes, until light and fluffy. If the buttercream is too thick, add more heavy cream. If too thin, add more confectioners' sugar until the desired consistency is reached.

Use immediately or store tightly covered in the refrigerator for up to 2 weeks.

VARIATION

VANILLA BEAN BUTTERCREAM

Substitute the vanilla extract with 2 teaspoons vanilla bean paste or half of a small vanilla bean pod.

VANILLA BEAN FILLING

MAKES 2 CUPS [380 G]

¾ cup [170 g] unsalted butter, at room temperature

2½ cups [250 g] sifted confectioners' sugar

1 vanilla bean (more or less, depending on size of vanilla bean and how speckled you want the filling)

Pinch of salt

In the bowl of a stand mixer fitted with the paddle attachment, cream together the butter, confectioners' sugar, scraped vanilla bean, and salt on medium speed until the sugar is incorporated. Increase the speed to high and whip for 6 minutes, until light and fluffy. Stop the mixer occasionally to scrape down the sides of the bowl. Chill the filling in the refrigerator for 45 minutes, until firm.

Once chilled, remove the filling from the refrigerator and place it between two layers of parchment paper, rolling it out to ⅛ to ¼ in [3 to 6 mm] thick. Carefully transfer the rolled-out filling (still between two layers of parchment) onto a baking sheet and freeze for 30 to 45 minutes.

Use immediately or store tightly covered in the refrigerator for up to 2 weeks.

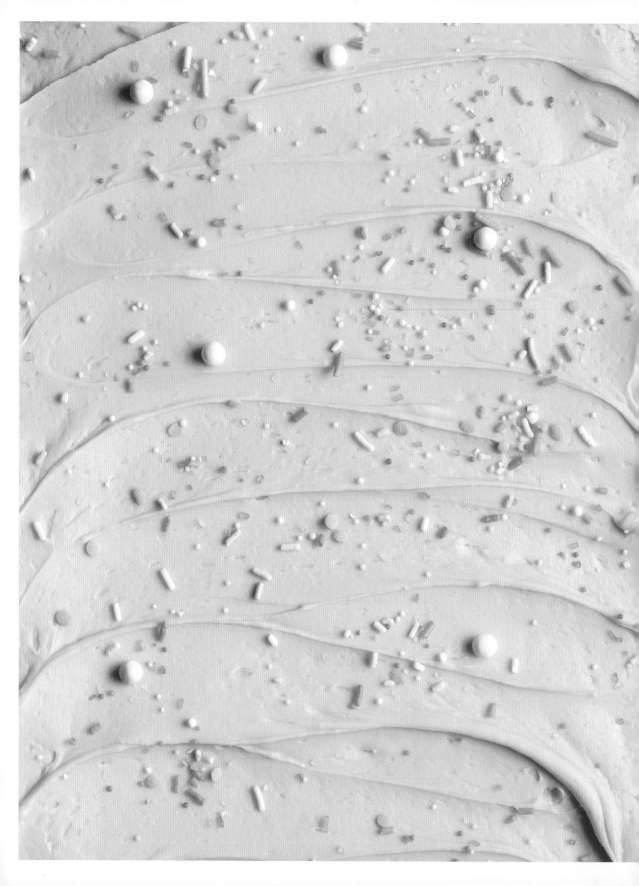

CAKE BATTER BUTTERCREAM

MAKES 2¾ CUPS [475 G]

½ cup [113 g] unsalted butter, at room temperature

1½ teaspoons clear vanilla extract (see Note)

Pinch of salt

3 cups [360 g] confectioners' sugar, sifted

Pink gel food coloring (optional)

1 to 2 tablespoons half-and-half

In the bowl of a stand mixer fitted with the paddle attachment, beat the butter on medium speed for 1 minute. Add the vanilla and salt, mixing well to combine. Add the confectioners' sugar, 1 cup [120 g] at a time, until incorporated. Increase the speed to medium-high and beat for 3 to 4 minutes, or until light and fluffy. Stop the mixer and scrape down the sides of the bowl. Add the food coloring, if using, and mix well on low speed, adding more food coloring until the desired hue is reached. Add 1 tablespoon of the half-and-half. Beat on high speed for 1 minute until light and airy. If the buttercream is too thick, add more half-and-half.

Use immediately or store tightly covered in the refrigerator for up to 2 weeks.

Note: Clear vanilla extract can be found in most grocery stores near the regular vanilla extract, or on Amazon.

CINNAMON BUTTERCREAM

MAKES 3¼ CUPS [540 G]

½ cup [113 g] unsalted butter, at room temperature

3½ cups [420 g] confectioners' sugar, sifted

1 teaspoon vanilla extract

1 teaspoon ground cinnamon

Pinch of salt

1 to 2 tablespoons heavy cream

In the bowl of a stand mixer fitted with the paddle attachment, beat the butter on medium speed for 1 minute until light and creamy. Add the confectioners' sugar, 1 cup [120 g] at a time, mixing on low speed until incorporated. Stop the mixer and scrape down the sides of the bowl. Add the vanilla, cinnamon, and salt, mixing to combine. Increase the speed to high and mix for 3 to 4 minutes, or until light and fluffy, scraping down the sides of the bowl as needed. Add 1 tablespoon of the heavy cream and beat on high speed for 1 minute until the buttercream is light and airy. If the buttercream is too thick, add more heavy cream.

Use immediately or store tightly covered in the refrigerator for up to 2 weeks.

WHITE CHOCOLATE BUTTERCREAM

MAKES 3 CUPS [560 G]

½ cup [113 g] unsalted butter, at room temperature

5 oz [140 g] white chocolate, melted and cooled to room temperature

2½ cups [300 g] confectioners' sugar, sifted

½ teaspoon vanilla extract

2 tablespoons heavy cream

In the bowl of a stand mixer fitted with the paddle attachment, beat the butter on medium speed for 1 minute until light and creamy. Add the melted, cooled white chocolate and mix on low speed until incorporated. Slowly add the confectioners' sugar and mix on low speed until combined. Increase the speed to medium-high and mix for 1 minute. Stop the mixer and scrape down the sides of the bowl. Add the vanilla and heavy cream. Mix on low speed and then increase the speed to medium-high, mixing until light and fluffy.

Use immediately or store tightly covered in the refrigerator for up to 2 weeks.

ESPRESSO BUTTERCREAM

MAKES 2¾ CUPS [475 G]

½ cup [113 g] unsalted butter, at room temperature

3 cups [360 g] confectioners' sugar, sifted, plus more as needed

1½ teaspoons vanilla extract

1½ teaspoons fine espresso powder (not granules)

Pinch of salt

1 to 2 tablespoons heavy cream or whole milk, as needed

In the bowl of a stand mixer fitted with the paddle attachment, beat the butter on medium-high speed for about 3 minutes, until smooth and creamy. Stop the mixer and scrape down the sides of the bowl. Turn the mixer speed to low and slowly add the confectioners' sugar, ½ cup [60 g] at a time. Mix in the vanilla and espresso powder. Add the salt. Turn the mixer back up to medium-high speed and mix for 2 minutes until smooth. If needed, add 1 to 2 tablespoons of heavy cream, depending on your desired consistency. If the buttercream is too thin, add more confectioners' sugar. If too thick, add more heavy cream.

Use immediately or store tightly covered in the refrigerator for up to 2 weeks.

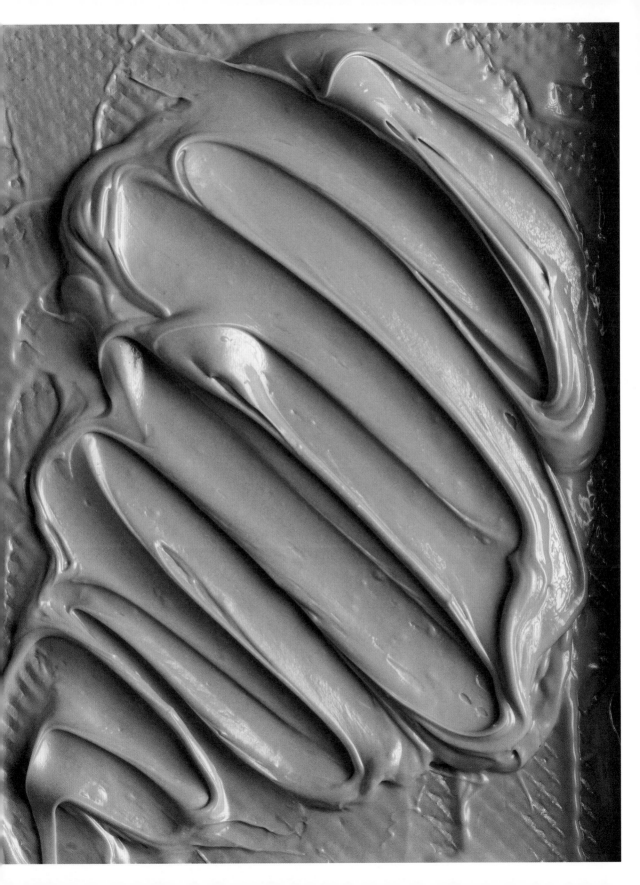

BROWN SUGAR BUTTERCREAM

MAKES 2½ CUPS [665 G]

10 tablespoons [145 g] unsalted butter

¾ cup [150 g] light brown sugar, packed

¼ cup [60 ml] heavy cream, plus more as needed

1 teaspoon vanilla extract

3 cups [360 g] confectioners' sugar, sifted, plus more as needed

In a medium saucepan over medium-low heat, bring the butter, brown sugar, and heavy cream to a low boil, stirring often.

Remove from the heat and stir in the vanilla. The mixture will splatter and foam. Transfer the mixture to the bowl of a stand mixer and let cool completely.

Add the confectioners' sugar, ½ cup [60 g] at a time, mixing on low speed until incorporated. Stop the mixer and scrape down the sides of the bowl. Then beat the mixture on medium-high speed for 2 to 3 minutes, until light and fluffy. If the frosting is too thick, add more heavy cream 1 tablespoon at a time. If too thin, add more confectioners' sugar.

Use immediately or store tightly covered in the refrigerator for up to 2 weeks.

GUAVA BUTTERCREAM

MAKES 3 CUPS [560 G]

½ cup [113 g] unsalted butter, at room temperature

3 cups [360 g] confectioners' sugar, sifted, plus more as needed

¼ cup [75 g] guava jam (see Note)

2 to 3 tablespoons heavy cream

In the bowl of a stand mixer fitted with the paddle attachment, beat the butter and confectioners' sugar on low speed until the sugar is incorporated and then increase the speed to medium-high for 1 minute. Add the guava jam and mix on medium speed for 2 minutes, until fully incorporated. Stop the mixer and scrape down the sides of the bowl as needed. Add 2 tablespoons of the heavy cream and mix on high speed until light and fluffy. If the buttercream is too thick, add more heavy cream. If too thin, add more confectioners' sugar until the buttercream is thick but easy to pipe.

Use immediately, or store tightly covered in the refrigerator for up to 2 weeks.

Note: Guava jam can be found in the jams and preserves aisle at your local market.

PUMPKIN SPICE BUTTERCREAM

MAKES 2¾ CUPS [550 G]

½ cup [113 g] unsalted butter, at room temperature

3½ cups [420 g] confectioners' sugar, sifted, plus more as needed

3 tablespoons pumpkin purée (not pumpkin pie filling)

¼ teaspoon ground cinnamon, plus more as needed

¼ teaspoon ground nutmeg, plus more as needed

Pinch of salt

1 to 2 tablespoons heavy cream

In the bowl of a stand mixer fitted with the paddle attachment, beat the butter for 2 minutes, until light and creamy. Add the confectioners' sugar in two additions, mixing on low speed until combined. Add the pumpkin purée, cinnamon, nutmeg, and salt. Mix on low speed and then increase the speed to medium-high and mix for 1 minute. Add 1 tablespoon of the heavy cream and mix for another 2 to 3 minutes, until light and fluffy. If the buttercream is too thin, add more confectioners' sugar. If too thick, add more heavy cream. Adjust the spices to taste.

Use immediately or store tightly covered in the refrigerator for up to 2 weeks.

EGGNOG BUTTERCREAM

MAKES 2½ CUPS [420 G]

½ cup [113 g] unsalted butter, at room temperature

2½ cups [300 g] confectioners' sugar, sifted

½ teaspoon ground nutmeg

¼ teaspoon ground cinnamon

Pinch of fine sea salt

1 to 2 tablespoons eggnog or heavy cream

1 teaspoon vanilla extract

In the bowl of a stand mixer fitted with the paddle attachment, beat the butter on medium-high speed for about 3 minutes, until smooth and creamy. Stop the mixer and scrape down the sides of the bowl. With the mixer on low speed, slowly add the confectioners' sugar in two batches. Add the nutmeg, cinnamon, and salt and mix to incorporate. Add 1 to 2 tablespoons of the eggnog, depending on desired consistency. Add the vanilla. Turn the mixer back up to medium-high speed and mix for 2 minutes, until the frosting is light and fluffy.

Use immediately or store tightly covered in the refrigerator for up to 2 weeks.

CHAI SPICE BUTTERCREAM

MAKES 2¾ CUPS [495 G]

9 tablespoons [130 g] unsalted butter, at room temperature

3 cups [360 g] confectioners' sugar, sifted, plus more as needed

½ teaspoon ground cinnamon

¼ teaspoon ground cardamom

Scant ¼ teaspoon ground allspice

Pinch of fine sea salt

1 teaspoon vanilla extract

1 to 2 tablespoons heavy cream

In the bowl of a stand mixer fitted with the paddle attachment, beat the butter on medium-high speed for about 3 minutes, until smooth and creamy. Stop the mixer and scrape down the sides of the bowl. With the mixer on low speed, slowly add the confectioners' sugar in three additions, followed by the cinnamon, cardamom, allspice, and salt. Mix in the vanilla. Add 1 tablespoon of the heavy cream. Turn the mixer back up to medium-high speed and mix for another 2 minutes, until smooth. If the buttercream is too thin, add more confectioners' sugar. If too thick, add more heavy cream.

Use immediately or store tightly covered in the refrigerator for up to 2 weeks.

PEPPERMINT BUTTERCREAM

MAKES 2¾ CUPS [475 G]

½ cup [113 g] unsalted butter, at room temperature

3 cups [360 g] confectioners' sugar, sifted, plus more as needed

¼ teaspoon peppermint extract

Pinch of salt

2 tablespoons heavy cream, plus more as needed

In the bowl of a stand mixer fitted with the paddle attachment, beat the butter for 30 seconds, until light and creamy. Add the confectioners' sugar in two additions, mixing on low speed until combined. Add the peppermint extract and salt. Increase the speed to medium-high and mix for 1 minute. Add the heavy cream and mix for another 2 to 3 minutes, until light and fluffy. If the buttercream is too thin, add more confectioners' sugar. If too thick, add more heavy cream.

Use immediately or store tightly covered in the refrigerator for up to 2 weeks.

BAILEY'S BUTTERCREAM

MAKES 2¾ CUPS [475 G]

½ cup [113 g] unsalted butter, at room temperature

3 cups [360 g] confectioners' sugar, sifted

2 tablespoons Dutch-process cocoa powder, sifted

1 teaspoon vanilla extract

Pinch of salt

2 tablespoons Bailey's Original Irish Cream liqueur

In the bowl of a stand mixer fitted with the paddle attachment, beat the butter for 1 minute, until light and creamy. Stop the mixer and scrape down the sides of the bowl. Add the confectioners' sugar, 1 cup [120 g] at a time, and the cocoa powder while mixing on low speed. Once the sugar is incorporated, add the vanilla and salt and increase the speed to medium-high. Mix for 2 to 3 minutes, until light and fluffy. Add the Bailey's and mix for 1 minute more.

Use immediately or store tightly covered in the refrigerator for up to 2 weeks.

TOASTED MARSHMALLOW FILLING

MAKES 4 CUPS [480 G]

3 egg whites [about 100 g]

¾ cup [150 g] granulated sugar

¼ teaspoon cream of tartar

Pinch of salt

Clean the metal bowl of a stand mixer with soap and water. Wipe it down with lemon juice or vinegar to remove any residue. In the bowl, combine the egg whites, sugar, and cream of tartar and whisk together. Set the bowl over a pot filled with 2 to 3 inches [5 to 7.5 cm] of simmering water, being careful not to let the bowl touch the water below. Whisking often, heat the mixture over low heat until the sugar dissolves and the mixture looks frothy on top. Using a thermometer to check the temperature, it should read 165°F [75°C]. Remove the bowl from the heat and place it directly in the stand mixer fitted with the whisk attachment. Add the salt. Beat on medium-high speed for 6 to 8 minutes, or until stiff peaks form and the bottom of the bowl is no longer warm to the touch. Use immediately or store tightly covered in the refrigerator for up to 2 days.

PEANUT BUTTER MOUSSE

MAKES 3¼ CUPS [635 G]

10 tablespoons [145 g] unsalted butter, at room temperature

6 oz [170 g] full-fat cream cheese, at room temperature

⅔ cup [170 g] creamy peanut butter, at room temperature

Pinch of salt

1 cup [120 g] confectioners' sugar, sifted

½ cup [120 ml] heavy cream

In the bowl of a stand mixer fitted with the paddle attachment, beat together the butter and cream cheese on medium speed until smooth and creamy. Add the peanut butter and salt and continue to mix until incorporated. Turn the mixer down to low speed and add the confectioners' sugar and mix until smooth. Stop the mixer and scrape down the sides of the bowl.

In a medium bowl, whip the heavy cream with a hand mixer on high speed until stiff peaks form.

Use a spatula to gently fold the whipped cream into the peanut butter mixture, being careful not to deflate the mousse.

Fill a piping bag with the mousse to use immediately or store tightly covered in the refrigerator for up to 2 weeks.

PEANUT BUTTER FILLING

MAKES 1¾ CUPS [360 G]

⅔ cup [170 g] creamy peanut butter, at room temperature

½ cup [113 g] unsalted butter, at room temperature

1 cup [120 g] confectioners' sugar, sifted

In the bowl of a stand mixer fitted with the paddle attachment, mix the peanut butter and butter on medium-high speed until smooth and creamy. Turn the mixer down to low speed and slowly add the confectioners' sugar. Mix until smooth and well combined. Stop the mixer and scrape down the sides of the bowl as needed.

Fill a piping bag with the peanut butter mixture to use immediately or store tightly covered in the refrigerator for up to 2 weeks.

PEANUT BUTTER FROSTING

MAKES 3 CUPS [765 G]

½ cup [113 g] unsalted butter, at room temperature

1½ cups [440 g] creamy peanut butter, at room temperature (not all-natural peanut butter)

2¼ cups [270 g] confectioners' sugar, sifted

2 to 3 tablespoons heavy cream

2 teaspoons vanilla extract

Pinch of salt (optional)

In the bowl of a stand mixer fitted with the paddle attachment, beat the butter on medium speed until light and creamy. Stop the mixer and scrape down the sides of the bowl. Add the peanut butter and mix on medium speed for 1 minute. Add the confectioners' sugar, ½ cup [60 g] at a time, while mixing on low speed. Once the sugar is incorporated, increase the speed to high and mix for 1 minute. Stop the mixer and scrape down the sides of the bowl. Add 2 tablespoons of the heavy cream and the vanilla. Mix on medium-high speed until light and fluffy, 2 to 3 minutes. If the buttercream is too thick, add more heavy cream. Add salt, if using, and mix to combine.

Fill a piping bag with the frosting to use immediately or store tightly covered in the refrigerator for up to 2 weeks.

MAPLE BROWN BUTTER FROSTING

MAKES 3½ CUPS [775 G]

1 cup [226 g] unsalted butter, at room temperature

2 oz [55 g] full-fat cream cheese, at room temperature

3½ cups [420 g] confectioners' sugar, sifted, plus more as needed

¼ cup [60 ml] pure maple syrup

2 teaspoons vanilla extract

Pinch of salt

In a medium saucepan over medium-high heat, melt ½ cup [113 g] of the butter, stirring only occasionally. Once the butter is melted, begin stirring often. The butter will crackle and pop as it browns, and it will start to foam slightly. Once the sizzling sound stops, continue stirring often until golden-brown bits begin to collect on the bottom of the pan. The butter will smell slightly nutty and turn a rich, amber brown. Remove from the heat, pour into a heatproof bowl, and allow to cool to room temperature.

In the bowl of a stand mixer fitted with the paddle attachment, combine the brown butter, the remaining ½ cup [113 g] butter, and the cream cheese. Beat for 2 minutes on medium-high speed, until light and creamy. Add the confectioners' sugar, 1 cup [120 g] at a time, mixing until incorporated. Beat for 1 minute on medium-high speed. Add the maple syrup, vanilla, and salt. Mix on low speed to combine and then increase the speed to high for 1 minute, mixing until fluffy. If too thin, add more confectioners' sugar.

Use immediately or store tightly covered in the refrigerator for up to 2 weeks.

BROWN BUTTER CREAM CHEESE FROSTING

MAKES 1¾ CUPS [390 G]

6 tablespoons [85 g] unsalted butter

4 oz [115 g] full-fat cream cheese, at room temperature

2¼ cups [270 g] confectioners' sugar, sifted

1 teaspoon vanilla extract

¼ teaspoon fine sea salt

In a medium saucepan over medium-high heat, melt the butter, stirring only occasionally. Once melted, begin stirring often. The butter will crackle and pop and foam slightly as it browns. Once the sizzling sound stops, continue stirring often until golden-brown bits begin to collect on the bottom of the pan. The butter will smell slightly nutty and turn a rich amber brown. Remove from the heat, pour into a heatproof bowl, and allow to cool to room temperature.

In the bowl of a stand mixer fitted with the paddle attachment, combine the brown butter and cream cheese and mix on medium-high speed for 2 to 3 minutes, or until smooth. Turn the mixer down to low speed and add the confectioners' sugar, vanilla, and salt. Turn the mixer back up to medium-high speed and mix for 2 to 3 minutes, until well combined and smooth.

Use immediately or store tightly covered in the refrigerator for up to 2 weeks.

VARIATION

CREAM CHEESE FROSTING

To make a basic Cream Cheese Frosting, don't brown the butter. Instead, simply use 4 tablespoons [56 g] room-temperature butter.

MEYER LEMON CURD

MAKES 1¼ CUPS [350 G]

1 tablespoon Meyer lemon zest (from 1 or 2 medium lemons)

3 egg yolks, at room temperature

5 tablespoons [70 g] unsalted butter, cubed

⅓ cup [80 ml] fresh Meyer lemon juice

¼ cup [50 g] granulated sugar

Put the zest in a medium heatproof bowl and place a fine-mesh strainer over the bowl. Set aside.

Place the egg yolks in another medium heatproof bowl.

In a medium saucepan over low heat, combine the butter, lemon juice, and sugar. Cook, stirring often, until the sugar is dissolved and the butter is melted.

Remove from the heat and slowly add the butter mixture to the egg yolks while whisking constantly.

Return everything to the saucepan. Cook over medium-low heat until thickened, stirring often.

When the curd has thickened enough to coat the spatula, strain it into the bowl of zest, using a spatula to push the curd through the strainer. The strainer will catch any bits of cooked egg. Clean your spatula and then use it to collect all the strained curd adhering to the bottom of the strainer.

Once strained, stir the curd often to allow the steam to escape as it cools. Let cool for at least 15 minutes on the counter. Once it is cool to the touch, transfer to a jar and place it in the refrigerator overnight. It will thicken as it chills.

Use immediately or store tightly covered in the refrigerator for up to 1 month.

KEY LIME PIE CREAM CHEESE FILLING

MAKES 2¼ CUPS [575 G]

4 oz [115 g] full-fat cream cheese, at room temperature

6 tablespoons [85 g] unsalted butter, at room temperature

1 tablespoon key lime zest

2 tablespoons fresh key lime juice

Pinch of salt

4 cups [480 g] confectioners' sugar, sifted

In the bowl of a stand mixer fitted with the paddle attachment, beat the cream cheese and butter on medium-low speed until pale and creamy, about 2 minutes. Add the lime zest, lime juice, and salt and mix on low speed until well combined. Add the confectioners' sugar, 1 cup [120 g] at a time, mixing on low speed. Once all the sugar is added, increase the speed to medium-high and beat for 2 to 3 minutes, until light and fluffy. Stop the mixer and scrape down the sides of the bowl as needed.

Use immediately or store tightly covered in the refrigerator for up to 2 weeks.

HONEY MASCARPONE

MAKES 1¾ CUPS [230 G]

4 oz [115 g] mascarpone, at room temperature

4 oz [115 g] full-fat cream cheese, at room temperature

1 to 2 tablespoons honey

In the bowl of a food processor fitted with the blade attachment, combine the mascarpone, cream cheese, and 1 tablespoon of the honey and pulse until combined. If desired, add 1 tablespoon more honey to taste.

Use immediately or store tightly covered in the refrigerator for up to 2 weeks.

WHIPPED MASCARPONE FILLING

MAKES 1¾ CUPS [230 G]

4 oz [115 g] mascarpone, at room temperature

4 oz [115 g] full-fat cream cheese, at room temperature

1 to 2 tablespoons fresh lemon juice

Salt and freshly ground black pepper

In the bowl of a food processor fitted with the blade attachment, combine the mascarpone, cream cheese, 1 tablespoon of the lemon juice, and the salt and pepper and pulse until combined. Add 1 tablespoon more lemon juice if the mixture is too thick.

Use immediately or store tightly covered in the refrigerator for up to 2 weeks.

WHIPPED GOAT CHEESE FILLING

MAKES 1¼ CUPS [255 G]

8 oz [230 g] fresh goat cheese, soft but slightly chilled

2 tablespoons extra-virgin olive oil

2 tablespoons fresh lemon juice

1 garlic clove, minced

¼ teaspoon kosher salt

In the bowl of a food processor fitted with the blade attachment, combine the goat cheese, olive oil, lemon juice, garlic, and salt and pulse until combined.

Use immediately or store tightly covered in the refrigerator for up to 2 weeks.

WHIPPED HERB CREAM CHEESE

MAKES 1¼ CUPS [350 G]

12 oz [340 g] full-fat cream cheese, at room temperature

2 to 4 tablespoons heavy cream or whole milk

1½ tablespoons finely chopped fresh dill or thyme

In the bowl of a stand mixer fitted with the whisk attachment, combine the cream cheese, 2 tablespoons of the heavy cream, and dill. Mix on medium-high speed for 2 minutes, until the cream cheese is whipped. Stop the mixer and scrape down the sides of the bowl as needed. You may have to add 1 to 2 tablespoons more cream to get the desired consistency.

Use immediately or store tightly covered in the refrigerator for up to 2 weeks.

CHIVE CREAM CHEESE FILLING

MAKES 1⅓ CUPS [300 G]

8 oz [230 g] full-fat cream cheese, at room temperature

3 tablespoons Greek yogurt

1 tablespoon fresh lemon juice

¾ teaspoon salt

¼ cup [10 g] finely chopped chives

In the bowl of a food processor fitted with the blade attachment, combine the cream cheese, yogurt, lemon juice, and salt and pulse until combined. Use a spatula to stir in the chopped chives.

Use immediately or store tightly covered in the refrigerator for up to 2 weeks.

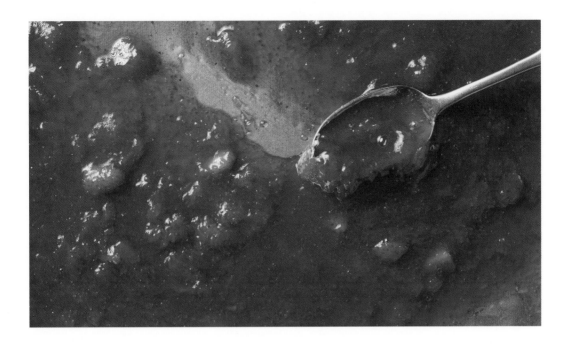

HOMEMADE STRAWBERRY JAM

MAKES 3½ CUPS [1 KG]

1 lb [455 g] strawberries, hulled and quartered

1¼ cups [250 g] granulated sugar

Zest of 1 lemon

¼ cup [60 ml] fresh lemon juice

Lemon seeds, secured in cheesecloth

Place a small glass dish in the freezer.

In a medium saucepan over medium-high heat, combine the strawberries, sugar, lemon zest, lemon juice, and the cheesecloth pouch of lemon seeds. Stir to combine. Once the sugar dissolves, continue to stir frequently as the mixture cooks for 15 to 20 minutes, or until the liquid thickens.

To check whether the jam has set, spoon a dollop of jam onto the frozen dish and return it to the freezer for 3 minutes. After 3 minutes, push the jam with your finger. If it ripples, the jam is done. If it does not, then return the dish to the freezer and continue to cook the jam over medium-high heat. Check again after 3 to 4 minutes.

Once the jam has set, remove the pouch of lemon seeds and pour the jam into a heatproof jar or bowl. Let cool at room temperature and then cover and place the jar in the refrigerator for at least 3 hours. It will thicken as it cools.

Use immediately or store tightly covered in the refrigerator for up to 3 months.

SLOW-CHURN VANILLA ICE CREAM

MAKES 5 CUPS [970 G]

1½ cups [360 ml] whole milk, cold

1¼ cups [250 g] granulated sugar

1½ tablespoons vanilla extract

Pinch of kosher salt

2½ cups [600 ml] heavy cream, cold

In a large bowl, combine the milk, sugar, vanilla, and salt and mix with a hand mixer on medium-high speed to combine well. Add the heavy cream and mix for 1 minute. Cover and refrigerate for 3 hours or overnight.

Stir the mixture and then churn it in an electric ice cream maker according to the manufacturer's directions. The ice cream will be soft and creamy.

Line a 9 by 13 in [23 by 33 cm] baking dish with wax paper.

Once churned, transfer the ice cream to the prepared baking dish. Use a spatula to spread the ice cream into the corners of the pan and level the top.

Freeze overnight or until solid.

Store tightly covered in the freezer and use within 2 months.

VARIATIONS

BOURBON ICE CREAM

Using the vanilla ice cream base recipe, decrease the granulated sugar to 1 cup [200 g] and add ¼ cup [50 g] packed light brown sugar. Stir 2 to 3 tablespoons of bourbon into the ice cream mixture before refrigerating and churning.

CHERRY ICE CREAM

Place 1½ cups [180 g] pitted cherries in a blender (or use an immersion blender) and blend until the fruit is puréed. Strain the purée through a fine-mesh strainer, reserving the juice. Discard the purée. Stir the juice into the chilled vanilla ice cream base just before churning it in the ice cream maker. Use a sharp knife to quarter an additional 1½ cups [180 g] pitted cherries and add them to the ice cream maker during the last few minutes of the churning cycle.

CHOCOLATE CHIP ICE CREAM

Add 1 cup [140 g] finely chopped milk or dark chocolate near the end of the churning cycle, about 5 minutes before the ice cream is ready.

CINNAMON ICE CREAM

Add 2 teaspoons ground cinnamon to the vanilla ice cream base.

CLASSIC CHOCOLATE ICE CREAM

Decrease the granulated sugar in the vanilla ice cream base to ⅓ cup [65 g]. Add ⅓ cup [65 g] packed light brown sugar and ¾ cup [60 g] Dutch-process cocoa powder, sifted.

COCONUT ICE CREAM

Decrease the amount of heavy cream in the vanilla ice cream base to 1½ cups [360 ml] and add one 14 oz [400 g] can cold coconut milk. For added flavor and texture, add 1 cup [80 g] unsweetened shredded coconut during the last few minutes of the churning cycle (optional).

CONFETTI ICE CREAM

Stir ½ to ¾ cup [80 to 120 g] rainbow sprinkles into the churned ice cream before freezing.

MINT CHIP ICE CREAM

Add 1 cup [140 g] finely chopped milk or dark chocolate and ½ to 2 teaspoons pure peppermint extract (depending on your desired strength of flavor) near the end of the churning cycle, about 5 minutes before the ice cream is ready.

THANK-YOUS

Writing this cookbook has truly been a team effort, and it would not be complete without a huge and heartfelt thank-you to all of the people who made it possible. It was an honor to be given the opportunity to share my tried-and-true recipes in these pages, and I could not have done it alone.

To my agent, Andrianna Yeatts at ICM: Your support, advice, and unwavering excitement for this book has made all the difference. I knew I was in the best hands from the moment we met. You believed in me from the start and for that I am forever grateful. Thank you for keeping me on task and on time throughout this journey.

To the team at Chronicle Books: Working with you has been a dream come true. To my editor, Claire Gilhuly, I appreciate your attention to detail, your expertise, and most of all your patience in helping me create the book I've always dreamed of. It has been a joy to work with you to bring this book to life!

Lizzie Vaughan, you have captured my vision for this book beautifully. Thank you for shaping my words and ideas into something better than I could have imagined. You have gone above and beyond to make each and every page of this book shine.

To Jason, my all-around favorite person: You are always there for me when I need an extra dose of encouragement and have cheered me on through many late nights of editing and writing. Thank you for being my number one fan and for keeping me company in the kitchen. I am grateful to have you by my side every step of the way.

To my girls, Avery, Ella, and Alden: Thank you for enthusiastically tasting *all* the cookies. I know this book is good because it has your stamp of approval! You inspire me to be the best mother, wife, friend, and baker that I can be. The three of you are my greatest blessings. This book, and everything I do, is for you. I hope I've taught you that with a lot of hard work (and a little luck), all of your wildest dreams can come true!

Mom and Dad, thank you for *everything* but especially for giving me the confidence to believe I can do anything. Because of you, I can! You are the very best cheerleaders a girl could ask for, and I am so lucky to call you wonderful humans my parents!

To my sister, Lisa: Thank you for being the glue that holds our family together and for being the very best auntie while I was busy in the kitchen. I love you and appreciate you more than you'll ever know.

To Alda and Suzie: Your dedication and steadfast commitment to all of the behind-the-scenes work you do does not go unnoticed. I could not have made this cookbook without you. Thank you for keeping the wheels turning on the blog while I poured my whole cookie-loving heart into this book. I am so grateful our paths have crossed, and I thank you for enthusiastically sharing your time and talent.

To my taste testers—neighbors, friends, family members: Thank you for being so willing to consume copious amounts of cookies and for your valuable feedback. Every note and comment made this book what it is today.

To my friends near and far who have checked in with me while I've been buried in sugar and flour 24/7 for months on end: Thank you, *thank you*! Thank you for being there for me when I need it most and for making space for me to laugh and cry, sometimes all at once. You all are my favorite people to bake for, and I look forward to sharing freshly baked cookies with you for years to come.

And lastly, thank you to the readers of *Browned Butter Blondie* for baking my recipes in your kitchens and sharing them with the ones you love. Your encouragement means the world to me. This is all for *you*!

—H.

INDEX

STUFFED

Chronicle Books publishes distinctive books and gifts. From award-winning children's titles, bestselling cookbooks, and eclectic pop culture to acclaimed works of art and design, stationery, and journals, we craft publishing that's instantly recognizable for its spirit and creativity. Enjoy our publishing and become part of our community at www.chroniclebooks.com.